As a leader in the telecommunications industry, our job is to make extraordinary connections through our network. Oftentimes, our "network" is only considered through the lens of technology, and we know that "extraordinary" connections are only possible by expanding the definition to our people and our partners. The "extraordinary" happens when this human network of employees and partners is seen as one in the same—built on trust and aligned values, common goals, and accountability across all functions. _Partnering Success_ is a force multiplier. Theresa's experience and best practice outlined in this book will enable "the extraordinary" in your business.

– Keri Gilder, CEO, Colt

I've read countless books on partnerships, but none have left a lasting impression quite like _Partnering Success_ by Theresa Caragol. Her approach is refreshingly practical, yet profoundly impactful. Theresa's emphasis on trust, shared vision, and mutual success resonated deeply with me. This book isn't just about forging partnerships; it's about building relationships that stand the test of time. If you're serious about driving innovation and growth through strategic collaborations, _Partnering Success_ is a must-read.

– Rob Rae, CVP of Community and Ecosystems, Pax8

In a world where partnerships are often seen as mere transactions, *Partnering Success* stands out as a guiding light towards genuine, enduring relationships. Not only is Theresa Caragol the master at building trust and authentic relationships, but her approach is both enlightening and empowering. This book provides both the "what" and, more importantly, the "how" of building successful partnerships. I 100 percent recommend reading this book!

– Andrea Sittig-Rolf, Chief BlitzMaster & CEO, BlitzMasters

Theresa Caragol's *Partnering Success* is a game-changer in the world of business partnerships. Her insights are not only enlightening but also actionable. As someone who's navigated the complexities of partnerships for years, I can attest to the transformative power of Caragol's framework. Whether you're a seasoned professional or just starting out, this book offers invaluable guidance for building dynamic partnerships that drive innovation and growth. Don't miss out on the opportunity to revolutionize your approach to partnerships with *Partnering Success*.

– Kelley Steven-Waiss, Chief Transformation Officer, ServiceNow

Partners are challenged, now more than ever, to respond to a complex industry which makes this incisive and inspiring blueprint a must-read for anyone looking to supercharge their business growth strategy.

– Todd Thibodeaux, CEO, CompTIA

In *Partnering Success*, Theresa Caragol makes it easy to understand how to build successful business partnerships—relationships that transcend transactions and embrace innovation. Successful leaders recognize the need to build strategic alliances that drive mutual success. Caragol's insights offer a compelling vision for the future of partnerships, including real-world examples of how to collaborate to win together. This book isn't just a read; it's a call to action for enterprises to rethink their approach to partnerships and to embrace a more innovative and prosperous future.

– Elizabeth A. Vasquez, CEO and Co-Founder, WEConnect

PARTNERING SUCCESS

THERESA CARAGOL

PARTNERING SUCCESS

THE FORCE MULTIPLIER TO ACHIEVE
EXPONENTIAL GROWTH

 | Books

Published by Advantage Books, Charleston, South Carolina.
An imprint of Advantage Media.

ADVANTAGE is a registered trademark, and the Advantage colophon is a trademark of Advantage Media Group, Inc.

Printed in the United States of America.

10 9 8 7 6 5 4 3 2 1

ISBN: 978-1-64225-758-8 (Paperback)
ISBN: 978-1-64225-757-1 (eBook)

Library of Congress Control Number: 2024910927

Book design by Megan Elger.

This publication is designed to provide accurate and authoritative information in regard to the subject matter covered. It is sold with the understanding that the publisher is not engaged in rendering legal, accounting, or other professional services. If legal advice or other expert assistance is required, the services of a competent professional person should be sought.

Advantage Books is an imprint of Advantage Media Group. Advantage Media helps busy entrepreneurs, CEOs, and leaders write and publish a book to grow their business and become the authority in their field. Advantage authors comprise an exclusive community of industry professionals, idea-makers, and thought leaders. For more information go to **advantagemedia.com**.

To the ultimate partners—mentors:
Bob O'Malley, Ron Rohner, and Karen Slatford

CONTENTS

ACKNOWLEDGMENTS

This book is a token of appreciation to my mentors, sponsors, and inspirers.

In this book, I distill a lifetime of passion for collaboration, partnerships, and the unleashing power of trust. This work is a tribute to our clients and partners who you see featured throughout with incredible wisdom, and our team at AchieveUnite—distinguished and genuine trailblazers committed to creating a significant, positive impact. A special thank you to two incredible AchieveUnite contributors, friends, and partners—Jessica Baker and Fiona Coughlan. I would also like to extend a heartfelt thanks to Jane Donaldson and Kira Jaramillo.

To my boys AJ and Sammy who I learn so much from every day, my husband Drew, and brother Jack and his family, Mom and Dad—you are my WHY.

I hope this book gives you insights that elevate both your professional and personal landscapes, fostering long-term relationships and partnering prowess. A special thank you to our advisors who have helped shape the work we do. I hold the powerful belief that communities and organizations like Baptie Communities, CompTIA, Alliance of Channel Women, WBENC and WEConnect, Informa, Partnership Leaders, and The Channel Company all have contributed greatly to the service of our industry segment. THANK YOU!

And to echo my friend Mike Schmidtmann's eloquent words: "Partnering is the new frontier of sales—Sales 3.0!"

FOREWORD: BOB O'MALLEY

"In a world bursting with new technology, how much more innovative can you be if you reach out to share others' developments? Why limit productivity advances to what your firm can do alone? Why not be even more efficient, for example, by adapting others' know-how or building a larger-scale plant with a partner? More generally, why not seek excellence by focusing on those things your firm does best and working with others in areas where they excel? Can you afford to lose such opportunities?"

These words were written by Jordan Lewis over thirty years ago in his book *Partnerships for Profit*. Since these words were written, business solutions have become more complex, requiring more diverse capabilities and new skills to deliver them. If the words and the implications were appropriate years ago, they are even more appropriate today, and most appropriate in the future where we will likely continue to see rapid rates of change.

After twenty years with IBM working with partners and clients in many capacities, I was fortunate to operate as CEO of several organizations, all involving partnerships in some form. In each situation, as the supplier and provider of products, I believed that I had the dominant role in my partner relationships. I never fully understood the partner's view until I retired from full-time work and started a collaboration with Theresa Caragol. Only then did I realize that the power had shifted from suppliers to the community at large and the partners.

Over the last eight years, Theresa, her teams, and I have worked with all sizes of organizations, on all kinds of partnering relationships, and in all parts of the world. We saw firsthand, in our engagements and training sessions, the need to come at the partnering process totally different from the way it had always been practiced. The playing field had leveled, and the game needed to be played differently.

Using the motto "Customers for Life" as a guide, we asked ourselves, "Why not partners for life?" So, Theresa created the Partner LifeTime Value® model, which has in turn resulted in the Partnering System for Success.

While Theresa's background is in technology, she realized that the Partnering System needs to be applicable to all industries and all kinds of partnerships. In the System for Partnering Success pages that follow, you will see the three related forces that are essential to developing long-term, mutually beneficial partnerships. These partnerships can be:

- Suppliers and Customers, and vice versa

- Suppliers and Integrators, and vice versa

- Integrators and Customers, and vice versa

They can be initiated from the demand side of the relationship or the supply side. In the following pages, you will see what these three forces are and how they interrelate, and how they must evolve for success.

The other realization that Theresa discovered in her work at AchieveUnite is that every partnership intersection is unique. Most organizations treat their partnerships with one brush. It is much easier for these organizations to standardize the terms of their partnerships, legally, financially, and operationally. At best, the terms might work for one partner, certainly not all.

On the contrary, each of the partners views their own business requirements as unique. In this book, Theresa advocates for an ecosystem approach that builds configurable partnerships, contract terms, flexible support models, and mutually determined success outcomes. She offers several diagnostics that can be applied to find the best partnering connection with each partner. These partnering tools are designed to deliver effective partnering with an adequate level of commonality.

CEOs, CFOs, and CROs will see a path to strengthening partnerships with a well-documented strategy and plans. They will have the confidence to commit the organization to partnering as the optimum approach to defined growth opportunities. Partner managers and sellers will understand how they can enhance their personal partnering quotient and learn the subtle techniques to earn a seat at the executive table.

As often said about a strategic initiative, it is a journey, not a destination. In the case of the System for Partnering Success, it is both a destination and a journey.

WHY DO YOU NEED A STRATEGIC PARTNERING SYSTEM?

In this book, we redefine partnering in the fast-paced business arena, emphasizing the necessity for a strategic partnership system. You'll learn how a proactive partnership strategy can transform your company's trajectory, impacting everything from internal culture to market reach and accelerating your company sales growth. This is a blueprint for building dynamic, enduring partnerships that will fuel innovation and drive success for your organization. If you have been, or are already, partnering in your business world, this book will help diagnose exactly how your organization can optimize your organization and achieve a 10× growth rate!

Just what is strategic partnering? Why do I need a system for it? And why now?

We live in an increasingly globalized world. Thanks to the increasingly fast evolution of tech and AI, we can work internationally with real, and sometimes automated, collaborators. Therefore, being able to fast track trusted and successful partnerships is more urgently needed now than ever before for successful short- and long-term growth. In the fast-paced, high-stakes game of modern business, it's evolve or die. The old transactional playbook of partnerships no longer applies; the "you scratch my back, I scratch yours" ethos is about as cutting edge as a flip phone in a world of smartphones. We are currently at a tipping point for collaboration, where the next move could either catapult us into a stratosphere of success or leave us scrambling in the dust of those daring to innovate their approach to strategic alliances, routes to market, and partnering overall. The challenges we face—from technological disruption to global sustainability—demand collective intelligence and joint action. Partnering has become imperative for every organization on the planet operating in the business-to-business (B2B) market.

In this book, we will look at partnering with an entirely different lens. We're going to look at the tangled web of partnering ecosystems, and how no company can afford to "go it alone" or ignore influencers and agents, marketplaces, strategic partnerships, and/or other novel ways to build relationships and accelerate organizations' success and growth.

We're going to demonstrate exactly why partnering is the most powerful growth strategy that any business can follow, offering you new tools in your partnering toolboxes, with the hard data to back these strategies.

This book presents a transformative strategy for enhancing investment yields through the concept of "partnering investment." It distills this into a practical framework, advocating for robust business relationships built on trust to achieve an optimized Partner LifeTime Value®. The core premise is simple yet profound: prioritize people, then partner businesses, and, finally, the collective entity, to forge enduring and mutually rewarding partnerships. This method is more than a business tactic—it's a commitment to sustained, value-driven partner relationships that promise long-term benefits for all involved.

Partnerships let you share resources, tap into new customer bases, and even split risks, so big ventures don't feel so daunting. And if you are already working with partners, we'll show you how to amplify those results with critical strategies. We'll also show you how you can build better partnering cross-functionally inside of your organization that will yield results internally and externally; for instance, in role progression up the career ladder, and externally in terms of profitable sales and business outcomes. Why stick to the slow lane, building everything from scratch, when you can team up with others, share the load, and speed down the fast lane together? Your partnerships are like jet fuel on the fire of innovation, igniting revolutionary products and services that disrupt markets.

It's about architecting a system that is fluid, flexible, and fearless—a formula that is as much about culture as it is about contracts. This system is about helping every person in your organization, your partners, and clients learn of your commitment for partnering success, so you can amplify your business tenfold by creating a culture of partnering in and across organizations.

In the heart of this book lies my unshakable belief that the spirit of partnership can be a catalyst for change. It has the power to redefine the landscapes of business and human interaction in our era. Partnering isn't just an external strategy; it's a culture that, when fostered within the very fabric of an organization, creates ripples that extend far beyond its walls.

This volume is more than a collection of insights. It reflects the stories shared by mentors, colleagues, and partners, illustrating the pivotal elements of successful collaborations. The incredible team at AchieveUnite embodies this ethos—authentic, exceptionally bright artisans of partnership, dedicated to the collective well-being—and establishes AchieveUnite Inc. methodologies as the best practices for partnering success. You will read stories and examples from small businesses, from individuals in the case of partnering, and from medium and large organizations that have mastered some of these best practices.

My aim is for this book to become a source of wisdom that bolsters your business partnerships and enriches your personal connections. When you cultivate the culture of partnerships in everything you do, within your organization and among your teams, the impact inevitably flows outward, influencing every external interaction with a force that can propel your business to new heights.

Join us in a journey to partner better with clients, partners, suppliers, and colleagues. Elevate your sales and business effectiveness. Become the best version of yourself as a success consultant, a collaborative coach, a strategic and trusted advisor. Partnering is the way of the future.

Through case studies, anecdotes, interviews, and exercises we will help navigate the System for Partnering Success, and the three essential dimensions:

- *Relationship Development*

- *Business Acceleration*

- *Community Orchestration*

Through the exercises and key next steps in each chapter, you can optimize your system for Partnering Success or build your system if you don't have one.

The Future Without a Partnering System

Consider a future without "Partnering Growth DNA," that is, one where your company has resisted change and maintained a static approach to partnering. Here's what may be happening in this imagined scenario, or if you are partnering already, but not getting the results you want:

- *You're suffering from stagnation and loss of competitive edge:* As others innovate and pivot, your company's offerings become outdated, leading to a gradual erosion of market share and influence. You may have some partners, but they are not performing at the level you expected.

- *You're also isolated in a connected world:* Without the advantages of a rich influencing ecosystem of strategic alliances and partnerships, your company struggles to expand, facing barriers that competitors effortlessly overcome through their collaborative networked ecosystems.

- *You're vulnerable to disruption:* Inflexibility and lack of diversity in thought and action leave your company vulnerable to economic shocks, technological disruptions, employee challenges, and shifting consumer behaviors.

- *You have missed many opportunities for growth:* The opportunities that arise from shared visions and cooperative efforts are missed, leaving your company trailing behind as others capitalize on these ventures.

- *Your brand may be taking a dive:* A company that is seen as behind the times struggles to attract and retain top talent, especially when the best candidates seek dynamic, forward-thinking, and collaborative work environments.

Contrast this with a successful partnering future, where your growth rate is a hockey stick, where you have created a flywheel of influencers and referrals, and people are talking about the work you do and the quality of your organization all over the place when you are not anywhere near the room nor any of your employees are present. It's a world where you are known as a company that cares, that puts customers and partners first, and that focuses on the win-win in everything you do. It could be a finance person and business development person collaborating, a new partner you are recruiting—in all cases people and organizations are building for short- and long-term win-wins.

The contrast between these two futures should be incredibly telling. Implementing a dynamic system for partnering is more than about simply keeping pace; it's about setting the pace. It's about recognizing that the future belongs to those who are bold enough to dismantle the silos, build bridges, and foster ecosystems of innovation and mutual success.

The choice is not between change and stability, but between transformation and obsolescence.

SYSTEM FOR PARTNERING SUCCESS

PARTNERING NORTH STAR

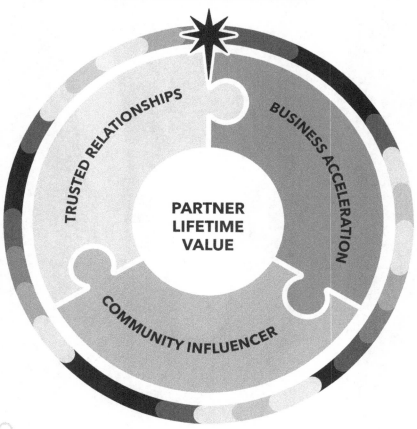

PART 1

THE SYSTEM FOR PARTNERING SUCCESS

CHAPTER 1

SEVEN CORE PRINCIPLES FOR SUCCESSFUL PARTNERING ECOSYSTEMS

The partnering imperative (Strategy and Policy), the three dimensions, and Partner LifeTime Value® combined make up the System for Partnering Success. There are some critical fundamentals to consider. Below we will unpack Seven Partnering Fundamentals underpinning the system, before proceeding to the Three Dimensions within the system itself.

Principle 1: Embrace That There Is Now a Science and a System to Partnering Success

When you adopt and follow this model, you and your organization will generate:

- *faster growth*

- *a higher return on your investment*

- *more sustainable profits*

- *accelerated productivity*

- *higher rates of innovation*

The system for partnering success (referred to throughout the book as SPS) is defined as:

SYSTEM FOR PARTNERING SUCCESS

PARTNERING NORTH STAR

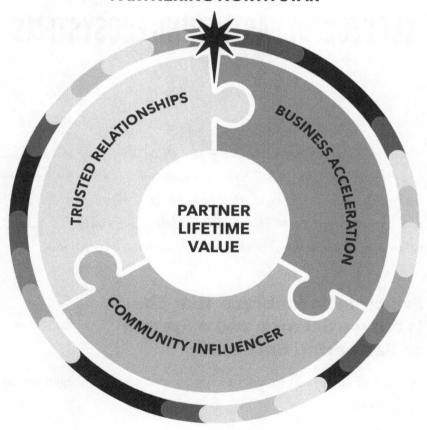

In this book, each of the three dimensions is a factor in partnering success leading to Partner LifeTime Value®. According to our research with the University of Glasgow, High Partner LifeTime Value® organizations are more successful overall, with higher partner revenue, higher rates of innovation and profitability, and higher revenue overall than those organizations that only leverage partnering and channels as a hobby.

Principle 2: Partnering Starts at the Top

Partnering commitment needs to be at the highest levels of the organization for three primary reasons:

1. *Ecosystem partnering requires all functions*—finance, legal, marketing, sales, and product—to be successful. It is not a sales function; it's a company strategy and policy. This means that organizations don't allow battles between people but instead encourage productive debate so that when escalations occur, it's a norm because everyone is trying to get to the right answer for the common good.

2. *Successful collaboration externally and internally across the organization is critical for successful partnering.* This means that everyone lives "work life" and "daily life" going about their business seeking to understand the company and partner's best interests, curious and open to disagreeing and debating dissenting opinions, and always seeking win-wins in every collaboration.

3. *Once the course is established, the organization must stay on it and not lose momentum.* Once decisions are made, everyone aligns around them. And once a "right answer" from a company is given, everyone sticks together in that right answer! That means hallway conversations and backroom

disagreements stop, and people move on to the next thing at hand.

Sure, partners provide short-term value-enhancing revenue generation, opening new markets, and offloading support services. The partnering potential, however, is far greater when you make a true long-term commitment to partnering.

François Locoh-Donou is the CEO of F5—a multi-cloud application services and security company—and Lisa Citron leads channels and partnerships. The company has been historically loved and valued by its partners. They have a long history of trust with their partners. They have a motto: transparency creates great partnerships. Francois said, "It's a core element of our way of working. You must lean into hard conversations and genuinely care about the person and the outcome. We have a 'Human First' and 'High Performance' culture at F5, and this extends to how we work with our partners. It's an essential tenet of how we do business together. This philosophy and partner-centric DNA have been a cornerstone of our success as a company." Lisa shared, "We are a partner-first company with virtually all our business conducted with partners. Healthy and productive partnerships are a critical cornerstone of our success as a company."

Principle 3: Partnering Works from the Outside-In

Partnering starts with the customer first. This is because success begins with a need; perhaps a vertical market application, a customer solution, an improvement opportunity, or services need of an organization.

It starts with a customer's need. Partnering happens to fulfill that need. If there is no need, there is no money or influence ability, and there is no customer whose requirements create the opportunity to partner. The reason for partnering is driven by a customer need for a solution that requires multiple parties, or it's an opportunity to create a customer need that perhaps never existed before.

I met Cameron in Year One of the AchieveUnite Next Gen Partnering Summit in Dulles, Virginia. The entire AchieveUnite team was so impressed with his humility, his openness and transparency, and his interest in learning from everyone—even though he works for one of the biggest and most influential companies in the world. Cameron's example below highlights this outside-in mentality.

> *Cameron Chehreh, head of United States Public Sector at Intel Corporation, believes that having a deep external perspective is essential for every team member in an organization. He challenges his team and others to continuously look outside and seek out opportunities to learn from customers, partners, and teammates in other functions. He emphasizes that this market and world is changing so fast that we must innovate, drive value together, and continuously lean into change. Cameron is also a champion of creating opportunities and structures to learn: third-party-hosted events and roundtables, including partners and customers in his own events, surveys and listening tours, interviews with clients and partners. He believes that he and his teams must always seek ways to listen and learn from the market. He shared that in the value chain as a business owner, you define clearly your beginning and end of the product/service you offer to customers. In order for your piece of the value chain to be delivered, it requires partnership, trust, governance, and a complementary business model to ensure the price = value*

equation is understood. Managing the quality of service delivery via partnerships and trust is critical to drive the customer experience within the ecosystem.

Principle 4: Partner Experience and Customer Experience Are Equally Important

An internet search of the term *customer experience* returns almost fifteen times more responses than *business partner experience*. Yet, in a B2B world, they are equally important. If you consider that partners oftentimes have influence with hundreds of customers, and exceptional partner experience delivers exceptional customer experience "on steroids," that means if you deliver exceptional partner experience, you will have 10× the number of customers, 10× the value of one customer, and 10× the satisfaction in a customer. This really is the core of what Partner LifeTime Value is all about.

Leading-edge research by Norma Watenpough and Nancy Ridge, members of the Association of Strategic Alliance Professionals, reveals that optimizing partner experience involves helping partners optimize their Customer LifeTime Value. This means organizations should focus on enhancing both partner and customer experiences equally to gain significantly more loyalty from both groups.

> *"Companies must find ways to create experiences that delight customers [and partners] through the fusion of humanity and tech."*
>
> —TIFFANI BOVA, *THE EXPERIENCE MINDSET* (NEW YORK: PENGUIN RANDOM HOUSE, 2023)

Principle 5: Partnering Trust Becomes a Way of Life—The Fundamental Ingredient to How You Approach All of Your Business

Partnering becomes a way of life and how you as a person approach your world, and how you interact with others. Historically, those who have been successful at partnering are also successful with other interpersonal relationships in their life. They might, for example, be good at partnering outside business settings, and just get along with their peers. Successful business partners might even be said to "go the extra mile, or get things done."

François Locoh-Donou, mentioned earlier, is an example of a *natural*. He approaches his relationships with great personal care, and he cares deeply about helping his colleagues and friends achieve their goals, leveraging his resources wherever it makes business sense. He activates the ecosystem flywheel by creating momentum and influencing others through doing good and doing good business. He values all his partners, customers, suppliers, and employees as critical to success for his ecosystem.

Ecosystem Community of Influencers

In our research and working practices over the last seven years, involving thousands of interviews and surveys from around the world, we asked respondents to describe the top qualities of their best partners. Our research shows that *trust* is number one—*more than 80 percent of respondents had trust as the top quality of a good partner.* Trust is the foundation for the next two qualities that respondents rated highly: being growth-oriented and engaged/collaborative.

According to Keri Gilder, CEO of Colt Technology Services:

"Businesses must be intentional in redefining their partnership strategy. Be upfront, accept and understand your business's gaps, shortfalls, and pain points, and be very clear around where you need partners to help you, your employees, and your customers to succeed.

As a leader, it's your responsibility to make it easy for people and organizations to partner with you, and that comes down to creating a partner-first culture. Role model openness, transparency, and trust; connect, listen, and create the space for a partner ecosystem to evolve and grow.

A successful longstanding partnership needs more than a common goal. If it's built on mutual values of trust and integrity, it will flourish."

Principle 6: Partnering Is a Key Skill, and Development Must Be Embedded for Every Team Member, Especially the Front Line of Organizations

Partnering is a core professional skill and value, and it is critical to the success of all salespeople, business developers, partner managers, technical team members, leaders, and other professionals, particularly those at the front lines of organizations. Dr. Catherine Lido, professor of Psychology and Adult Learning at the University of Glasgow, advocates that fast-tracking successful partnership, via Partnering Trust, should therefore become embedded into university curriculums across the globe, particularly for business and entrepreneurship. Partnering Trust development will pioneer the way we curate business relationships online and in person in the fast-track future of flourishing businesses. It is critical to develop and deploy empirically supported strategies, in order to positively direct how business gets done over the coming years.

At AchieveUnite, Fiona Coughlan, the beloved PPA educator, refers to this as the Tri Partnership Model. It means that partnering becomes a way of life for the sales teams, the partner teams, the engineers if it is a technical organization. Customer service and client success teams all understand partnering at a deep level and practice every day those skills with their teams, customers, and partners across the organization. And finance, legal, product, HR, and other supporting functions align around partnering competencies.

> *"Companies who take the time to understand their ideal partners obtain 50 percent more revenue from these partners because they deeply understand the partner's business model and priorities, and because they have educated their whole organization on how to best support these partners. These organizations build a deep competency in organization trust building."*

—ACHIEVEUNITE'S PARTNER LIFETIME VALUE EBOOK

Principle 7: Partnering Moves from Being a Low Priority in Your Organization to Becoming a Robust and Iterative Cornerstone of Your Company's Growth Strategy

Exponential, long-term partnering success requires a shift in mindset and partnering. AchieveUnite Inc. refers to this as Partner *LifeTime Value*®: the exponential value received by partners over the life of their partnering relationship. It doesn't matter if it's partner to customer, partner to partner, partner to supplier, or partner, supplier, and customer. The principle is there is an exponential gain from partnering that happens when organizations, teams, and people are self-sustaining, focused on mutual benefit, and align around growth and scalability. The outcome of Partner LifeTime Value is exponential growth, more sustainable growth, more productive growth, more inclusive and healthy growth.

Successful partner lifetime value partnering requires a deep understanding of your partner's needs.

Frank Picarello has seen partnering firsthand from many angles. He was a manager in service delivery organizations, a COO for three small business technology integrators, and the architect of small business solutions for a major networking company. When tasked with introducing new services for small businesses, he knew exactly what to do. He approached the opportunity from the partner's eyes. He put himself in their shoes and asked, "What is it they need *to grow their business and achieve their goals overall?" He then worked everything back from that.*

Our System for Partnering Success will give you exponential growth as well as a multiplier effect, as it has done for so many of the organizations we've worked with across industries and across tech including a software as a service company (SaaS), Security and Hyperscaler suppliers, and business partners. It will act as an engine propelling your organization and your priority partners forward. Watch your people grow, your company thrive, and your partnerships and customer relationships evolve into engines for growth and innovation. There are three critical dimensions to the AchieveUnite System for Partnering Success.

CHAPTER 2

THE THREE DIMENSIONS AND YOUR QUANTUM LEAP

The First Dimension: Trusted Relationship Building

Think about the people in your life who have made a positive impact. They could be family, teachers, coaches, or friends. And what is one thing these people have in common? You trust them. The same is true for successful partnering—it all starts with people who are empowered and trustworthy.

Does this sound like you? If so, you are a natural! You approach your relationships with great personal care, and you care deeply about helping your colleagues and friends achieve their goals, leveraging their resources wherever it makes business sense. You activate the flywheel by creating momentum and influencing others by doing good and doing good business.

Strong "naturals" connect dots and drive creativity and innovation together with their partner. They care about their partner's success along with their own and constantly look for ways to help their partner. Think of the best people you work with repeatedly. Do you see similar characteristics?

"After completing PQi in a bootcamp with industry colleagues, I can immediately see how accelerating trust drives acceleration of business! It's like a speed boat at full throttle."

—ANDON LUCAS, VP OF SALES, IMPERIUM DATA

"Since completing the PQi assessment and workshop, it is amazing the difference I can see in my team's engagement, morale, and thoughtful communication."

—DALYN WERTZ, EXECUTIVE DIRECTOR, PARTNER PROGRAM AND PARTNER MARKETING, COMCAST

What if you're not a natural? The good news is that there is now a science behind how to build partnering trust. The concept of a Partnering Quotient index (PQi) will be introduced. With a PQi assessment, you will understand your partnering profile strengths to build your partnering behaviors. You will get better relationships, stronger win-win solutions, and speedier business outcomes.

Partnering trust is the key ingredient underpinning every successful organization. If you can speed partnering trust, you can speed revenue, you can speed customer loyalty, and you can speed the success of your key business partnerships.

Tiffany Dunn, North American Partner and Alliance Leader at Autodesk, and John Muscarella, Channel Chief at Cox Business, were uncertain about the value of this psychometric assessment for their teams, and when introduced to PQi, they expressed similar concerns. However, through their assessment and interactions with a PQi coach and facilitator, they discovered that they had a dominant trust-building style that was enlightening to them both. Going forward, Tiffany thought about ways to leverage PQi to have different conversations with people depending on their trust-building style. Tiffany witnessed her team's excitement from their 2024 sales kickoff, where the team was introduced to PQi and participated in PQi workshops. Since she began using PQi for her team, she saw stronger collaboration, problem-solving, and communication, which she believes will translate into increased sales results and go-to-market efforts. Tiffany's skepticism turned to advocacy as she discovered the transformative impact of PQi on her team's performance and morale, proving that fine-tuning trust styles can unlock new realms of collaboration and achievement. As for John, he and his sales enablement team embedded PQi into their overall partnering skills building program that his company invested in for his teams, and they increased their skills significantly in client and partner trust-building, executive relationship building, and overall partner growth development.

The Second Dimension: Business Acceleration

The second dimension—Business Acceleration—underscores the imperative of embedding the culture, structure, policies, and programs deep within the company's DNA to build growth at scale. This is not just theory; it's practiced wisdom that has created companies everyone aspires to align with.

If you want your organization to be successful at partnering, it must go beyond the individual and team personalities and look at all company interactions. To develop a strong partner-centric growth culture, leaders need to set up the structures, processes, and programs to support the partnering growth strategy within all functions of the organization.

This kind of partner-centric growth culture, when done right, is a force of nature. It creates companies that everyone wants to be associated with. And it creates teams that are more productive and innovative. Imagine—faster and more sustainable growth, better business results, a great place to work, and amazing relationships that last for years to come. If you have an organization that is not a partner-centric growth organization, it is missing a huge accelerator opportunity, a real opportunity to improve the company's internal teamwork and employee satisfaction overall. You can quickly see the connection between partner-centric growth organizations that partner well with customers, partners, and suppliers and partner-centric growth organizations that collaborate extremely well on the inside!

After hundreds of interviews from our extensive work with clients of all kinds over the last six years, it was revealed that satisfaction with partnering varied significantly. For example, satisfaction with the partner's sales function was 50 percent higher than its marketing counterparts (25 percent), averaging at about 75 percent. Satisfaction with other supplier functions (like finance, product, or legal) was 10 percent lower than marketing at 15 percent. That means instilling the partnering-centric growth culture across the organization is essential and has ripple effects for employee cross-functional collaboration and overall employee satisfaction.

Another survey of one hundred executives by AchieveUnite Inc. involved in B2B partnerships discovered that these executives are 50 percent more likely to view partnering success through their own organization's lens, and not the lens of the partner's view on success. In other words, these executives viewed a successful partner as one who sells more of its products, *as opposed to a partner growing its own business.* In most cases, suppliers did not even know the status of the partner's business and financials.

Here's an example of a partner-centric growth company that yielded big results:

> *Rob Rae, the former visionary Global Partner Leader at Datto, architected a game-changing partnering strategy that became the lifeline of the company's triumph. "For us at Datto, partnering wasn't merely a strategy, it was our identity—the very essence that pulsed through the organization's heart," Rob asserts. This approach wasn't superficial; it was a deep-rooted ethos that influenced every layer of the company, fostering a culture of authentic collaboration and mutual respect.*
>
> *Under Rob's guidance, Datto transformed into an entity that didn't just do business with others but cared deeply about their success as if it were their own. "It was about empathy, about truly hearing our partners and responding not just adequately, but extraordinarily," Rob reflects. This led to actions and messages that resonated deeply, creating a ripple effect of trust and reliability at every interaction.*

The result of this profound partnership philosophy? A staggering network of twenty thousand loyal partners worldwide and a landmark $6.2 billion acquisition by Kaseya. "We didn't just grow; we evolved together with our partners, earning the esteemed title of the most trusted ally in the industry," Rob concludes, marking the legacy of a strategy that redefined the concept of success through partnerships.

Yes, the product, component, or services you offer or procure are important; this new world though demonstrates that real stickiness and differentiation come from the partnerships with clients, partners, and organizations who work with you and leverage the best of what you offer with what they offer.

- Do you regard the best companies you work with in business?

- How do you view your partnership with them? *Transactions to meet quarterly targets, relationships to build for the long run?*

- What would change if you could bring the same "best" partnering experience to all your relationships, internally and externally?

Winning feels good. In great partnerships both organizations and teams (if partnering internally) benefit and win. A "Partnering for Success" mindset focuses on value and on providing a win-win for everyone. When done right, the result is delighted customers, partners, and colleagues. You and your partners help solve real problems to deliver unique, innovative solutions to your shared customer. The *AchieveUnite System for Partnering Success* will transform how you approach relationships, how your organization approaches partnering, and help you 10× achieve your goals.

The Third Dimension: Community Orchestration

Here we discuss the strategic art of cultivating a vibrant partner and influencer community—a pivotal subset of the broader business ecosystems. This dimension serves as a guide to creating and participating in a thriving network and ecosystem of relationships where shared visions, learning, and collective growth are not just ideals but practiced realities. Here, we decode how to nurture common interests, foster collaborative learning and strategic intersections, and accelerate growth through the flywheel ecosystem.

You will work to master Community Orchestration, where your business is an integral part of a broader, interactive network. Think of it as being in a dynamic dance with fellow organizations. In this space, partnerships are more than mere alliances; they are a fusion of shared interests, goals, innovation, and collective aspirations. You will tackle how to navigate the complexities of this ecosystem, turning external market shifts and regulatory updates into strategic advantages. It's about fine-tuning your influence within the community to ensure your partnerships are resilient and robust. It is about private and public ecosystems, selecting and building and/or participating in the right communities in the ecosystem for your organization and partners' success. Picture your business as a vital node in an energy grid, with each partnership adding to the circuitry, empowering the whole network. Together, you're not just weathering storms; you're creating a renewable source of business energy.

Identifying and participating in these communities/ecosystems are critical to building and maintaining Partner LifeTime Value®.

Sure, the product, component, or services you offer or procure are important, but the real stickiness and differentiation come from the relationship with individuals and organizations that work with you.

"A primary value in communities is the sharing of experiences amongst the peers. The members need to set the agenda, with support from their partners. That's where the real growth and influence happens."

ROD BAPTIE, CEO, BAPTIE AND COMPANY–PRESIDENT AND CHAIR

Time to Evaluate

So—where are you now on the partnering spectrum?

Rate yourself, your organization, and your partners on the following scale of 1–10, with 10 being the highest.

Ask Yourself

Relationship Development	Rate yourself between 1 and 10, with 10 being the highest	How can you improve Relationship Development?
I am viewed by my peer associates as one who cares about their success more than I care about my own.		
I am curious and constantly seek to understand my partners' business drivers.		
I am confident enough to ask my partner executives relevant, but seemingly elementary, open-ended questions.		

Business Acceleration	Rate your organization between 1 and 10, with 10 being the highest	How can you improve Business Acceleration?
The successful profitable growth of our business partners is high on my organization's priorities and values.		
The functional leaders in my organization (VPs of Finance, Sales, Marketing, Product Development, Legal, HR) often interact with partner CEOs on business and personal levels.		
We celebrate the top-line and bottom-line growth of our partners as much as our own.		

Community Orchestration	Rate your industry between 1 and 10, with 10 being the highest	How can you influence Community Orchestration?
Solution component providers in my industry are stable and well established.		
We support and actively participate in peer communities led by our partners.		
Solutions in my industry that are delivered to the point of "use, purchase, or consumption" are well defined and have been for three or more years.		

What insights into your organization's present state of partnering have you gained from this exercise?

_____

_____

_____

_____

Key Takeaways from Chapter 2

- Successful partnerships are not just about aligning sales efforts; they are a holistic strategy involving all organizational functions—finance, legal, marketing, sales, and product development. It's a top-down strategy. You must have an unwavering commitment from the highest levels of leadership to embed a culture of collaboration both internally and externally and to maintain momentum once strategic directions are set.

- Trust is the primary quality for your successful partnerships. It underpins growth orientation and collaborative engagement. This focus on trust is essential for speeding up revenue, customer loyalty, and the success of key business partnerships.

- In the B2B context, your partner experience is just as critical as the customer experience. Partners often influence multiple customers, thus amplifying the impact of their experiences. Creating a partner-centric culture within an organization ensures that this positive influence reverberates through the customer base. The emphasis is on transforming the art of partnering into a daily practice, woven into the very DNA of the company, which in turn elevates internal collaboration and boosts overall business performance.

Partnering Road Map–Action Steps

1. *Ensure that the commitment to partnering starts at the top.* You should establish clear policies and rules of engagement around partnering that are supported and actively promoted by senior leadership. This includes setting up cross-functional teams that include members from finance, legal, marketing, sales, and product development to foster a cohesive approach to partnerships.

2. *You must begin to invest in training and development* programs that focus on building trust among team members, partners, and customers. Utilize tools like the Partnering Quotient index (PQi) to assess and improve trust-building skills within the organization. Encourage open communication, transparency, and mutual support to foster a culture where trust is the norm.

3. *Develop a partner-centric approach* that prioritizes the partner experience as much as the customer experience. Implement feedback mechanisms to regularly assess the satisfaction of partners and act on the insights gained. Recognize that a positive partner experience can lead to an amplified customer experience, so be sure to design partner engagement programs that aim to deliver value and satisfaction to both partners and customers.

CHAPTER 3

STRATEGIC PARTNERSHIPS–YOUR QUANTUM LEAP CONTINUED

In the dynamic world of business, strategic partnering muscle will serve as your organization's quantum leap factor for growth, innovation, and competitive advantage. However, jumping into partnerships without proper assessment can lead to pitfalls and unmet expectations. This chapter delves into the key indicators and processes for evaluating whether your organization is ready to embark or expand on a partnering journey.

Imagine standing at the brink of a new frontier, where the only ticket to entry is the audacity to partner strategically. That's where we are in today's lightning-paced business arena—poised at the edge of possibility. This chapter is your map to that new world, guiding you through the exhilarating process of creating partnerships that could redefine your organization's future.

The Heart of the Alliances, Channels, and Partnerships

Think of strategic partnerships as the lifeblood of modern commerce. They're not just handshakes between businesses; they're heartbeats syncing up to pump out breakthroughs, reach, and scalability that no single entity could achieve alone. But with high stakes come high risks—misalignment and cultural clashes can be the Achilles' heel of even the most promising unions. Dive deep into the anatomy of these partnerships to discover if your organization has the muscle to succeed in this endeavor.

Embedding a robust partnering framework within a company's DNA can lead to a 50 percent increase in productivity.

–STUDY CONDUCTED BY ACHIEVEUNITE IN COLLABORATION WITH THE UNIVERSITY OF GLASGOW

In this chapter, you will embark on a quest to uncover the ingredients that make partnerships not just work but flourish. You will explore how aligning visions can turn separate entities into market conquerors and how the blending of cultures can lead to a fusion of innovation.

Are You Ready Internally?

The journey begins with introspection, and then some hard-hitting work with your C-suite and management.

- Do you have a customer need or opportunity for partnering? In every single organization AchieveUnite has interacted with, the answer here has been YES.

- Does partnering align with your organization's long-term goals and strategy? This alignment is critical to ensure that partnering drives your business forward in the intended direction.

- Do you have the necessary staff, technology, and financial capacity to invest in this venture? Partnerships should not strain your resources but rather complement them.

- Do you have a culturally ready organization? Your organization must be open to collaboration, adaptable to change, and capable of integrating with the culture of the organizations you've identified as potential partners. The success of partnerships will hinge on this cultural alignment.

Collaboration between companies with differing cultures presents its own set of challenges. The company must develop strategies to overcome these challenges and create an environment conducive to collaboration. This may involve training programs and workshops designed to prepare staff for the changes ahead.

The commitment to integration is a significant step toward successful partnerships. This involves integrating systems, processes, and cultural elements, which may require establishing dedicated teams to manage this transition smoothly.

Can you build a company (or at least division-wide) commitment to partnering? Affirming partnering through a wide commitment is essential. This could involve signing preliminary agreements that reflect the company's dedication to cultural readiness and adequate resource allocation, thereby setting a strong foundation for success.

The Goals and KPI Alignment Connection– Measure What Matters in Partnerships

Of course, partnerships without clear metrics are like sailing without a map. You might catch a good wind, but you're just as likely to drift off course. That's where goals and key performance indicators (KPIs) come in. They're not just numbers on a dashboard; they're the key to making sure the partnership efforts pay off.

Note: Goals and KPIs are one model of metrics that we use at AchieveUnite. Other models like milestones and objectives and key results (OKRs) work as well—the key is the ongoing and rigorous goal setting and reviewing frequently so it becomes a weekly regular habit in your world.

In today's business world, there is no such thing anymore as the "trust me, it'll work" approach. Boards, investors, and teams expect to see results. Goals and KPIs are that proof. They show you where you are nailing it and where it's time to tweak strategies.

Leverage KPIs to effectively manage partners and the partner initiative and program.

1. Formalize objectives

2. Identify key metrics (leading and lagging)

3. Establish systems to capture, integrate, analyze, and track data

4. Ensure data capture policies and processes are implemented and followed

5. Leverage insights from data to enhance partner performance and evolve the partner program

Custom-fit your metrics. Each partner type and partnership is its own separate trajectory, with its own goals and challenges. Your goals and KPIs need to fit the partnering strategy like a glove. Whether you are looking to break into new markets or cook up the next big thing, it's critical to measure the right thing. It's also critical that you build a set of leading and lagging KPIs. What this means is that some of your metrics are "leading indicators or activity-based metrics" that you know if done successfully will give you the lagging indicator of success like new customers, quarterly and annual sales, and revenue growth.

Partnering KPIs

- Leading indicators—activities that facilitate reaching your objectives

- Lagging indicators—results directly related to reaching your objectives

Choosing the right goals and KPIs is about nailing down what success looks like for you and your partners, and then getting down to the nitty-gritty:

- *Strategic Alignment*—Goals and KPIs need to be in lockstep with what partners are aiming to achieve together.

- *Keep Them Clear*—If a goal leaves anyone scratching their heads, it's out. They've got to be crystal clear.

- *Make Them Countable*—If you can't count it, you can't use it. Simple as that.

- *Set the Bar High*—Ambitious, yet attainable—that's the goal sweet spot.

- *Stay on Point*—KPIs must keep up with developments in the market and stay relevant.

- *Check the Pulse Often*—Use goals and KPIs that take the organization's pulse—quickly and regularly.

Governance and Reporting: Steer the Partnering Ship with Great Goals and KPIs

Governance isn't just a fancy word for boring meetings. It's about steering the ship together and making sure you are headed in the right direction. Goals and KPIs are the compass that keeps things on course, ensuring everyone's pulling their weight, and that milestones are in place to achieve the goals.

KPIs have their quirks, though. It's easy to get caught up in the numbers game and miss the big picture. The key is to stay focused on action. Metrics should drive to do better, not just fill out reports. And when things change—as they always do—be ready to adjust KPIs, so they keep working for and not against the organization. "KPIs need to align at the global level for the partnering model, at the region or vertical level, and then individually with each partner and team who owns partnering," said Micheal McCollough, former chief partner officer at Akamai and Imperva. "It's like an orchestra that must be in harmony for a fantastic performance."

Critical success factors for KPI reporting, dashboards, and analytics for the company's partnering initiative, for the partners specifically, for your sales teams, and the partner program must all align.

Follow the steps below to ensure success:

1. Establish reporting RASCI

2. Identify key metrics (leading and lagging)

3. Determine data requirements

4. Analyze data availability/sources

5. Analyze capabilities to capture, integrate, and report data

6. Assess policies, processes, and behavior enablers and inhibitors (human)

7. Develop a plan to mitigate gaps in systems capabilities and policy/process compliance

"Partnering success requires a company initiative for partnering; it is foundational for realizing the investment."

–ACHIEVEUNITE'S PARTNER LIFETIME VALUE EBOOK

So, here's the bottom line: KPIs are the lifeline of any thriving partnership. Get them right, and they're like a lighthouse guiding you to success. Let's make them the tools that turn your shared visions into reality.

Remember, it's not about having KPIs for the sake of it. It's about having the right ones that tell you that you are winning the game with your partners. So, let's roll up sleeves, set some killer KPIs, and show everyone what can be achieved when together everyone is in sync.

For the partnering model to succeed, KPIs must be synchronized across all levels—globally, regionally, vertically, and individually with each partner and their respective teams.

Harness the Power of Your Data with Metrics and Dashboards

Current Partner **Program** Metrics Capabilities

 **Leading**

- Pipe by region
- Channel conflict
- Promos used
- Marketing Plans
- Forward business reviews
- Unified channel campaign adoption
- Available Staffing
- Product/Sales Training/Certification
- Channel Partner Resources

Lagging

- Bookings Growth/product/fami
- Booking new/renewal
- New Logos by Region
- Channel Conflict
- Renewal Rates
- Leads closed by campaign type
- Loss report

Navigate Risks and Exit Strategies

Understanding and managing risks are critical components of any partnership. It's vital for you to identify potential issues early on and have strategies in place to handle them. Creating transparent agreements and defining KPIs are practical steps to ensure that all parties involved are aligned and the partnership stays on course. However, it's a reality that not all partnerships will succeed as expected. When outcomes fall short or objectives begin to diverge, having an exit strategy prepared can allow for a smooth transition out of the partnership, minimizing any potential losses or negative impacts.

Making the decision to enter a partnership should always be a careful, analytical process. Including key stakeholders in the decision-making process can provide a wider range of insights and foster greater overall support. For an added measure of caution, starting with a smaller pilot project can be a wise move. This approach allows both parties to evaluate the partnership in a real-world setting, testing the waters before diving into a deeper, more extensive commitment.

It's important to continuously ask yourself the following questions no matter where you are in the journey:

- Is your company prepared to invest or expand investment in a partnering strategy? And/or in this partnership?

- Why would this type of partner or this specific partner want to work with your company?

- What value will this partner or group of partners bring to your company?

- Why do you want to work with them?

- What value do they bring to you?

- What partnership models work best for the partner?

- What model works best for your company?

- How will you help partners achieve their growth goals?

Our systems, born from cutting-edge research, are designed to tap into every facet of partnering. It's about understanding the gears that drive successful collaborations and fine-tuning them to work in harmony. With these systems, you're not just facilitating partnerships; instead you nurture them to thrive and innovate together.

Key Takeaways from Chapter 3

- Identifying your "Why" for partnering is essential to building the right strategic partnerships.

- Deciding to enter into strategic partnerships requires more than just identifying a potential collaborator. It demands a deep understanding of your organization's readiness, a meticulous evaluation of potential partners, the value of partnering for all parties, and a clear strategy for managing risks and evaluating success.

- By approaching partnerships with thorough preparation in-house and strategic insight, organizations can forge alliances that are not only successful but also sustainable for the long run.

Partnering Road Map–Action Steps

1. *Conduct strategy and KPI workshops with your internal team responsible for partnering if you don't have a partnering model, and hold strategy review workshops annually or semiannually if you do have a partnering model.*

   Set up a workshop with your partner and executive team. The goal? To define what success looks like for your collaboration. Bring in people from different levels and departments. You want a mix of big-picture thinkers and detail-oriented doers. During this session, work out the strategic goals for partnering and agree on the KPIs that best reflect these ambitions. Remember, these goals and KPIs should be specific, measurable, and directly tied to the outcomes you care about.

2. *Assess your readiness to partner (your company must be ready to partner):*

   Use this checklist to determine if you have the answers to these partner readiness elements and how important you think they are in your business.

You can see the readiness element category and the status, which means:

A. Are you 1, 2, 3, 4, or 5 (1 indicates not ready to partner, and 5 indicates extremely ready to partner)?

B. Then what are your gaps if you indicated a 3 or below?

C. How important do you believe this is in your company (high—very important, medium—somewhat, and low—little importance)?

If you already have a mature partnering model, visit www.achieveunite.com/vmi to evaluate your partnering success with a deeper level analysis tool: Value Measurement index.

✓ Partnering Readiness Checklist

Readiness Element	Status 1-5	Gaps	Priority H/M/L
Customer Journey and Ideal Profile			
Mapped Role of Partner in Customer Journey			
Ideal Partner Profile			
Partner Business Proposition			
Partner Program Framework			
Partner Automation/PRM			
Partner Recruitment Plan			
Partner Capacity Model			

Partner On-boarding Plan		
Partner Enablement Offering		
Partner Marketing Offering		
Partner Sales Model and Rules of Engagement		
Partner Program Reporting and Metrics		

3. *Build/modify your goals and KPI dashboard.*

   Once you've agreed on your goals and KPIs, it's time to make them visible. Work with your IT or data team to create a shared dashboard. This isn't just any dashboard, though. It needs to be user-friendly, real time, and accessible to all relevant stakeholders. The idea is to have a central place where anyone, at any time, can see how your partnering strategy and partnerships are performing. Make sure to include trend lines and progress over time, not just static numbers. There are plenty of third-party platforms that exist specifically designed for this purpose.

4. *Schedule regular KPI reviews.*

   KPIs aren't set-and-forget. They're living, breathing indicators of your partnering pulse. So, calendar in regular KPI reviews. These could be monthly, quarterly, or at a frequency that makes sense for the pace of your business. For example, in the technology industry a quarterly business review used to be sufficient, but because of the pace of change and constant speed a monthly business review has become much more the norm. Use these reviews to celebrate wins, learn from misses, and iterate on your approach. Be prepared to pivot your KPIs if the market shifts or if new opportunities arise. The goal here is continuous improvement and adaptation.

The QBR+ Flywheel keeps pace

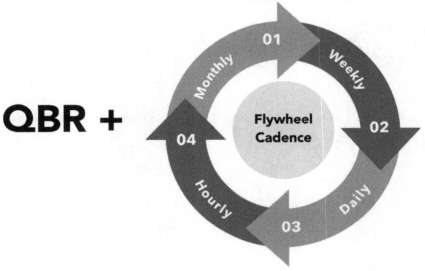

You'll find assessment worksheets for this chapter at https://www.achieveunite.com/partneringsuccessbookresources/.

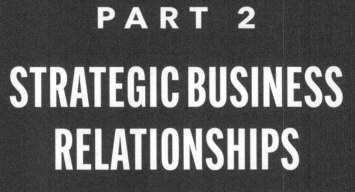

PART 2

STRATEGIC BUSINESS RELATIONSHIPS

INDIVIDUAL AND ORGANIZATIONAL TRUST-BUILDING FOR GROWTH

Contributors:
Dr. Catherine Lido and Gail Doerr

CHAPTER 4

PARTNERSHIP STRATEGY WITH PQi®

"Successful partnering is about building trust and rapport with your partner, understanding their needs, and working together to achieve common goals."

–HARBINDER KHERA, CEO, MINDMATRIX

In the prior chapters, you witnessed that building successful partnerships is key to successful business practice, and building trust is the foundation for such long-term flourishing partnerships. But once you have the strong foundations for trustful partnering, you might ask, can partnering trust be measured, and can you fast track this process? Our answer is a resounding Yes! This chapter presents PQi®, the Partnering Quotient index, tapping into the science of partnering trust.

AchieveUnite began working with companies in 2018 to improve their partnering strategies and capacities. The more we learned through our own work, the more passionate we became about researching and enhancing successful partnering as core to best business practices. We then began to wonder why some people and companies were more effective at building trusted partnering relationships than others.

We discussed this question with several technology executives who were really trying to figure this out. After volleying back and forth on whether it was the people or the company, we concluded that it was both, but needed the data to prove it.

The team at AchieveUnite began the quest to provide the missing piece of the puzzle. We embarked on a joint journey with academic collaborators to develop a scientific reliability and validated measure of the Partnering Quotient index (PQi). PQi is the first of its kind to scientifically quantify partnering trust in work-based scenarios, not just trust or partnerships on their own, using psychometric assessment, developed with subject matter experts and industry leaders.

PQi measures *how*, and *how effectively*, people build trusting partnerships. It was developed in conjunction with professors at Arizona State University, the University of Glasgow, and the University of Notre Dame. It works by offering metrics on one's dominant partnering strengths, thereby opening a dialogue about how you individually approach partnerships and shedding light on your "blind spots" in developing partnerships. Furthermore, PQi assessment tools identify opportunities to develop your weaker partnering areas, allowing you to strengthen your capacities and choose the best strategy for a partnering scenario. It also serves as a guiding light for teams to balance out trust-building styles and cross-company partnership teams to do the same.

PQi was designed to help you better understand the factors underlying your development of trustworthiness in partnering. This assessment leads to identifying whether you are effectively conveying to partners that you are competent, have their interests at heart, and will follow through on your promises. This self-awareness is then the first step in helping you improve your ability to develop and maintain trust-based relationships.

As Catherine Lido, PhD, University of Glasgow, UK, one of the PQi subject matter experts, states: "The AchieveUnite Partnering Quotient index, or PQi, applies statistical modeling to define, measure, and evaluate partnering in trust. PQi enables predictions about partnering successes in different applied contexts." "Trust is at the heart of all partnerships, and this is the first of its kind scientific measurement of trust." "PQi is the science of partnering. It's an indicator to the type of person you tend to be in the partnering scenario context. The five Profiles are tools in your toolbox that can strengthen your capacity. PQi applies statistical modeling to define, measure, and evaluate partnering trust. It enables predictions about partnering successes in different contexts," according to Dr. Lido.

PQi: A Comparison to Other Psychometric Assessments and Systems

Many progressive organizations use one or more psychometric assessments to develop their talent. While PQi is a perfect stand-alone system, it can also be a great complement for all of the other assessments. The most commonly used assessments include:

- Clifton's Strengths—Used primarily to help individuals and teams better understand their areas of strengths, develop their careers, and to teach leaders how to manage through strengths. From the assessment, individuals learn their top five strengths out of a possible thirty-four.

- Myers–Briggs Type Indicator—Helps individuals develop more self-awareness and better understand their behavior. It also helps them understand how they might differ from others. Individuals receive a "type," which is one of sixteen possible combinations of various qualities.

- DiSC—Used to determine an individual's work style so that they can better understand how to optimize their work and function better in their teams. Individuals receive a report that shows their two areas of greatest strength (e.g., Di or SC), with information about how strong they are in each.

How Is PQi Similar to Other Assessments?

Like most other assessments, PQi divides people into personality "types," which we call PQi profiles. It is similar in that it helps individuals become more aware of their areas of strengths, preferences, and behavior patterns. PQi, as with other systems, can help individuals to better understand others and help teams to develop a useful common language.

How Does PQi Differ from Other Assessments?

The following are key points of distinction for the PQi system:

1. PQi is the only assessment that specifically assesses trusting relationships, the foundation of all business and personal success.

2. The PQi assessment is highly evidence-based in terms of reliability and validity.

3. The PQi system is simple, straightforward, and accessible yet has profound and immediate impact on individuals, teams, and organizations.

4. There are only five PQi profiles to remember. Everyone has varying levels of competencies in each profile, with one or two showing up as the "dominant profile(s)."

5. PQi profiles can change over time and in different situations. When we change jobs or roles, mature in our roles, or shift job responsibilities, we might develop stronger competencies in the profile that best fits the new situation.

6. Unlike most other assessments, PQi offers strategies and tactics to develop greater competencies in your weaker areas of trust-building. These can be taught, reinforced, and used situationally to build trust.

7. All PQi experiences (workshops, coaching) address relevant, timely, industry-specific business challenges and are tailored for each client.

8. PQi supports organizations by addressing the "how" of meeting KPIs and ROI through trusting, effective, productive, and loyal relationships, both internal to the organization and externally with partners.

What Challenges Does PQi Solve?

The application of PQi in business can have far-reaching impacts for individuals, for teams, for your organization, and for your partners. And we also find people applying PQi to their personal lives and with their spouses, partners, and friends!

"Companies understand the need to develop trust within the organization. We often see leadership give a 'nod' to the importance of trust by conducting team-building exercises or holding 'get-to-know-you' events. Although these activities

can be fun, they often fail to accomplish their underlying goal of developing the skills necessary to build trust. PQi tackles trust-building head-on. It clearly identifies the traits and behaviors that will help employees build lasting relationships with coworkers, managers, and partners."

–JULIANNE ZUBER, SKILLSTORM PARTNERSHIP LEADER

Here is a set of use cases for PQi.
Check which of these applies to you.

- ▫ During my many integrations after we purchased a company there was a high level of conflict and fear.

- ▫ When I took over as CEO, and there were silos, the executives were not operating as a team.

I could have used a tool like this:

- ▫ To help accelerate my partners' and my sales teams' work together so we can get to solving the customer challenges faster. We all know speed matters.

- ▫ To drive higher cross-functional teamwork within my organization, especially when I took over a company that was a turnaround.

- ▫ To help me work with my partners, so they would be more transparent with me faster.

- ▫ To show my sales teams how to work more creatively with customers.

- ▫ To encourage teams to work better together and have much more trust and collaboration.

If you answer yes to any of these, PQi can help increase productivity, speed, and transparency.

Building and Accelerating Trust in a Virtual and Hybrid World

Building trust with team members, business partners, sales prospects, and customers is increasingly challenging in the digital world, where we might miss out on important social cues. As more companies have transitioned to remote and hybrid work post-pandemic, virtual meetings, virtual education, and virtual conferences may be the norm. As contact between others became confined to a computer screen, eye contact, body language, and nonverbal cues became much more difficult to process. Developing rapport and bonding with colleagues was suddenly happening in a completely different way. Therefore, people have begun to take a broader view of what collaboration means in online settings, and how to build trust with "virtual others," and more specifically, how to attain and sustain it when face-to-face contact is not possible.

Dr. Renee Pizarro, former global digital sales and commercial segment leader for Hewlett Packard Enterprise and entrepreneur, has used various assessments throughout her career to help her teams with emotional intelligence, conflict resolution, and cultural awareness, but she had never come across an assessment specific to trust that was backed by scientific research. She found it in PQi.

"We wanted to provide our digital sellers with another tool in their toolbox to help them understand how to establish trust in a virtual environment quickly," Dr. Pizarro says. "When you have in-person, face-to-face communication, there's a huge advantage with that instant energy and body language. But with a camera, it's not the same. The virtual world doesn't replace the real world even if you have a very high-end, interactive type of communication solution."

"PQi is a great tool that we've never had in my industry, a tool that shows you how to fundamentally teach trust. As a researcher myself, it was important to me that there was real science behind this assessment. That was the differentiator that set the AchieveUnite solution apart from everything else.

"You can use PQi to really enhance your connection to your customer," she says. "We put so much into the onboarding process around product information and technology and a lot of jargon. The reps get overwhelmed with information that they're not necessarily going to apply right away. But understanding how to establish trust and how other people establish trust is a skill set that they could apply immediately."

PQi®–The Assessment and Profile

Previous research into how personality impacts trusting partnerships in the workplace has been limited to date. Consequently, scholars have suggested that it would be helpful to uncover the individual differences that lead to more trusting relationships.[1] Our work on the PQi answered this call. PQi does not identify traits, as other personality assessments do. Instead, it helps people reflect on their underlying default partnering strategies, including underlying "neo-facet" traits, as well as social interactions, which lead to more trusting relationships and developing partner trust-building strategies they may be lacking.

"PQi was designed to help you improve trust-building behaviors and tendencies," said Michael Baer, PhD, professor at the WP Carey School of Business at Arizona State University, who was one of the early architects of PQi.

---

1   Mike Baer et al., "Uneasy Lies the Head that Bears the Trust: The Effects of Feeling Trusted on Emotional Exhaustion," Academy of Management Journal 58 (2014), https://doi.org/10.5465/amj.2014.0246.

Many personality tests used in the workplace are based on "typing" people, and seem to convey, "This is your personality." The message is "You're stuck with it, so get used to working around it." The PQi assessment improves upon personality assessments by acknowledging that you can develop more trusting partner relationships through increased social intelligence and self-reflection. Perhaps more importantly, PQi and its associated workshop experiences provide organizations with the tools to improve employees' trust-building capacities, both inside of their organizations and externally with their clients and business partners.

So, what does fast-tracking trustful partnerships entail? The PQi journey starts with a twelve-minute assessment, which can easily be done via an app on your mobile device, your tablet, or your laptop. You'll be asked to rate yourself on statements that best describe you in partnering situations.

The assessment measures your underlying default or "implicit" tendencies of thinking, feeling, and behaving in work-based scenarios—thereby assessing the relative strengths in five quantifiable domains.

Strategizer, Collaborator, Energizer, Exemplar, and Harmonizer

You receive a score for each profile and learn your dominant partnering strategy or strategies. You can then identify the profile that you most readily deploy in partnering contexts, the strengths, and blind spots of this approach, as well as those you are less likely to draw upon, and you may wish to develop.

You will likely have significant experiences and strengths within all the profile competencies, but you are probably most comfortable and accomplished in a dominant profile domain. It's very important to remember that none of the profiles are better than others. Each profile domain has strengths, values, and blind spots. Your profile identifies your tendencies, the places where you are most comfortable, often your starting points. Another way PQi is unique among other systems is that it can teach you to become more literate—strengthening competence—in the profiles that are less dominant for you. Ultimately, the goal is to become strong across all profile domains, and to have the ability to recognize them in others, thereby drawing upon the partnering tools most effective in the situation at hand. Now, I will never be strong at everything—however, this tool also helps with team building and balancing out trust-building across people and roles.

Now let's take a closer look at the five PQi profile domains. The chart below shows each of the five PQi profiles with a brief description of each.

PQi®: The 5 Profiles

Collaborator	"Teamwork makes the dream work."
Energizer	"Strangers are just friends we've never met."
Exemplar	"Anything worth doing is worth doing right."
Harmonizer	"Keep calm and carry on."
Strategizer	"Data first, theories second."

The PQi® Currency

We usually think about currency as money to exchange commodities and services. It typically applies to a business or personal transaction, based on money or bartering. In partnering and trust-building, we define currency as *an exchange based on a way of being.* In other words, a person demonstrates currency in their behaviors. The behaviors reveal what they have to offer others and what they can consistently deliver. This kind of currency is solidly rooted in a person's values and beliefs and cued by the situational context surrounding them.

When we look at the PQi profiles, we start to see that each profile has a foundational and dominant set of trust-building currency or currencies. Here are the five:

- *Strategizers*—Their currency is more likely rooted in data and information. Their partners can quickly see that they deliver on promises by demonstrating excellence in their work and by offering ample analysis and details to back up their ideas.

- *Collaborators*—They are more likely to partner based on cooperation, mediation, and service. In their work and partnerships, they consistently consider the good of the whole, not just the individual parts. They will be cooperative and agreeable and seek consensus whenever possible.

- *Energizers*—Their partnering mindset is rooted in strong charisma and rapport in relationship building. They can break through barriers in business by focusing on individuals and sensing what they need at any given time. They can also see or build connections between people, ensuring trusting bonds are built and nurtured.

- *Exemplars*—They are anchored in integrity and quality. Count on them to set and adhere to high standards. They will consider and promote equity in all relationships. They also can be counted on to be honest, even when the truth is hard to hear, which is one way they earn the trust of others.

- *Harmonizers*—They base their partnerships on rationality and calmness. They consistently bring a sense of ease to the environment and their relationships. They can deal with conflict and change without being emotionally triggered, which makes them a trusted asset in complex and challenging situations.

Knowing the underlying dominant "currency" with which the people you work with are operating allows you to better understand what they value, and what they can reliably and effectively deliver, as well as how you can best communicate for success. Additionally, knowing the currency of your partners, supervisors, peers, and employees helps you to manage and relate to individuals through a tailored, respectful, and more personalized approach.

> *"Through the PQi experience, our team accelerated productivity by at least 6 months, if not a year."*
>
> **–DALYN WERTZ, EXECUTIVE DIRECTOR, PARTNER PROGRAM AND PARTNER MARKETING, COMCAST**

Let's look at examples of how PQi can be used. Jim Chow is a well-known partnering expert and strategic alliance builder. He spent years at Google, studying partnerships and building growth relationships as a hobby. Jim is a Strategizer first, and second an Energizer. His lowest profiles are Exemplar and Harmonizer, although those are still strong muscles for him.

As a result of taking the PQi assessment, he is now focused on building his top strengths and understanding how he leverages them with others; and he is learning more about his weaker profiles and whether he wants to develop any of those muscles. Since taking PQi, Jim has also begun recognizing the partnering personalities of others.

So, Jim's scores look like this:

Strategizer	90.3%
Energizer	87.5%
Collaborator	84.7%
Harmonizer	83.3%
Exemplar	83.3%

Here's another example. Erica was a senior sales executive at a Fortune 100 technology vendor. She was a person who could build amazing relationships with certain people. However, with others, she really struggled. Together we talked about why she felt confident and successful in some situations and not in others. After doing our PQi assessment and profiling, we found the answer.

Erica was an expert at building trust as a Collaborator. She was agreeable, generous, and cooperative in her relationships and naturally sought out and considered diverse perspectives. She enjoyed working as part of a team and, during conflict, she was often able to find common ground. These are great qualities that Erica could continue to leverage. The profile where she scored the lowest was the Strategizer. The strengths for this profile are around analysis, details, spotting trends, and being able to break down complex issues. When Erica worked with partners who valued the Strategizer strengths, she found she just couldn't connect. Once Erica understood more about this, she was able to build her Strategizer muscle by creating tactics and showing behaviors that demonstrated those strengths.

Strategizer	75.3%
Energizer	82.5%
Collaborator	85.7%
Harmonizer	83.3%
Exemplar	79.3%

To a lesser degree, she also worked on the other profiles that were not dominant so that she eventually had a more complete "toolbox" to develop trust in a wide variety of situations and with partners and clients who valued or needed different approaches. It's important to note that each person rates themselves differently, and not to compare your scores to another person—instead compare your scores over time for yourself. Different people assess themselves differently based on backgrounds, culture, gender, and other factors.

Key Takeaways from Chapter 4

- Quantifying Trust in Partnerships: PQi, or the Partnering Quotient index, is a tool developed to scientifically measure the level of trust in business partnerships. It assesses how effectively individuals can build trust, a fundamental pillar in any partnership. By quantifying trust-building competencies, PQi provides actionable insights into how individuals and companies can enhance their approach to creating and maintaining successful partnerships.

- Personalized Development: The PQi assessment offers a unique opportunity for personal growth by identifying an individual's dominant trust-building strengths and areas for development. This personalized approach ensures that individuals can hone their skills in building trust, essential for successful collaborations. It encourages a more profound self-awareness of how one is perceived in terms of competence, concern for others, and reliability.

- PQi has a broad range of applications that can speed up productivity, team cohesion, and client relationships, leading to accelerated organizational growth. It provides a structured framework for individuals and teams to improve their trust-building strategies and, by extension, strengthen the entire organization's partnering capabilities. This can be particularly beneficial during times of change or when integrating new teams or partners into the company's ecosystem.

Partnering Road Map—Action Steps

1. *Conduct PQi Assessments Across the Organization.* Initiate a comprehensive assessment process using PQi for all team members involved in partnerships. This will help identify everyone's dominant partnering strengths and areas where they can improve. By understanding these profiles, the organization can tailor development programs to enhance trust-building skills effectively.

2. *Integrate PQi Insights into Training and Development.* Develop targeted training programs that address the specific needs highlighted by the PQi assessments. Focus on improving

individuals' weaker areas while also reinforcing their strengths. This can include workshops, coaching sessions, and collaborative exercises that align with the identified competencies of Strategizer, Collaborator, Energizer, Exemplar, and Harmonizer.

3. *Apply PQi to Partner Engagement Strategies.* Utilize the detailed insights from PQi profiles to inform and refine the organization's partner engagement strategies. This could involve adapting communication methods, negotiation tactics, and collaborative approaches to align with the trust-building preferences of both your team and your partners. By doing so, the organization can foster more robust and productive partnerships that are based on a solid foundation of trust.

CHAPTER 5

PQi® APPLICATIONS

M&A INTEGRATIONS AND INTERNATIONAL PARTNERING

PQi® as a Tool for Promoting Faster Integration During Mergers and Acquisitions

In the previous chapter, you learned about the groundbreaking approach of PQi®, and how it can be used as a tool individually for personal and professional growth, increasing your competencies for fast-tracking trustful partnerships in the workplace. But every week, you hear about companies merging or being acquired. You may have experienced firsthand how difficult it is to get two teams with different cultures and different styles to suddenly come together. Therefore, this chapter focuses on the usefulness of PQi at the team and organizational level, particularly when teams are facing rapid change or integration.

Trust-building is especially important during M&A integrations. And this is where PQi comes into its own as a valuable tool. PQi gives people a "common language" for partnering approaches, and the PQi workshop experiences, unpacked below, are a safe space to bring into the open the challenges and barriers they are having.

The specific leadership capabilities and qualities related to trust have a direct impact on business performance. For example, the *Korn Ferry Institute's research on organizational transformation revealed that 50 percent of the difference in financial performance among highly transformational companies over a five-year period was related to trust in leadership. It stands to reason that this trust differential also applies within teams and with external partners.*[2]

And this is where PQi comes into its own as a valuable tool. PQi gives people a "common language" and an advanced skill set for working through change and transitions. When people are able to normalize change and build trust simultaneously, they understand how to activate the strengths of each PQi profile in service to their organization, their teams, and the change initiative. They can also more accurately predict which team members or partners will resist or struggle with change and proactively apply meaningful interventions.

The PQi workshop experiences, unpacked below, intentionally create a safe environment to bring into the open the challenges and barriers they are having, individually and collectively. Participants also learn how to rely on and enhance each other's strengths.

We saw this in action when we were called in to work with a large technology software company that had acquired and merged with a smaller company. In confidential interviews with team members from both companies, we learned that there was little trust and a high level of fear as well as change fatigue. In the carefully tailored and facilitated

---

2   "KFI: Leadership Drives Success Drucker Partnership," Korn Ferry Institute, accessed June 16, 2024, https://www.kornferry.com/content/dam/kornferry-v2/pdf/institute/kfi-leadership-drives-success-drucker-partnership.pdf.

workshops, the groups began to explore the real issues preventing them from partnering effectively.

"The higher a company's success in partnering directly correlates to the partners' trust in the vendor and in the people of the vendor."

–ACHIEVEUNITE'S PARTNER LIFETIME VALUE EBOOK

One example, in the acquisition of Company B by Company A below, the challenge wasn't just in combining operations but in uniting people. Distrust and cultural clashes threatened to undermine the ambitious goals of the acquisition. The following case study showcases the transformative power of trust-building and strategic change management in turning two divergent teams into a cohesive, goal-oriented unit. It's an exploration of how understanding the human side of M&A is crucial for success in the modern business landscape. They each had their own assumptions and began realizing through the use of change models, role-plays, and small group work that these assumptions were not always correct. They also realized why their first reactions about the other company were not always correct—they were operating from their dominant profile's characteristics—and more specifically their blind spots. It was a very powerful experience for those in the sessions. By the end of our workshops with them, they better understood how to navigate change and how to respect and utilize each other's strengths. They also created a unified team purpose and actually started having fun together. All of this led to a more synergistic integration and a team of high collaborators and high contributors.

PQi® Case Study

Case: Merger and Acquisition:

Two teams coming together from Company A and Company B needed to achieve ambitious goals for sales, leveraging and merging their current clients, and successful processes.

Business Problem:

Individuals from Company A didn't trust that their counterparts in Company B were using best practices in sales and business. Instead, they expected them to completely adapt to the processes and practices of Company A.

Individuals from Company B saw that their unique business practices, based on deep relationships and strong customer loyalty, were not being considered or respected. They felt that Company A, the dominant culture, would "eat them up and spit them out." Only one month into the acquisition, many of them were preparing their resumes and planning to leave.

AchieveUnite Process:

As an independent third party who promised anonymity, AchieveUnite was able to learn, through insightful and candid interviews, the root of the issues.

To begin with, all the individuals completed the PQi Assessment. Summaries uncovered that individuals from both teams were resisting the imposed changes, which was evident in the way they worked together and whether they accepted their shifting roles. There was a severe lack of trust between the teams. Without addressing both issues, the goals of the M&A would not be achieved.

AchieveUnite Solution Experience:

As part of the experience, they would learn how to normalize the psychology of change using a widely respected model (William Bridges, *Managing Transitions*).

When the results of the PQi assessments were combined across both teams, collectively, 40 percent of the group were Strategizers. This meant that they build trust by sharing data, details, and discussing the "why" behind every decision. This was a good starting point because they could leverage this commonality. At their core, Strategizers are normally slower to build trust, but there were enough of them to create a critical mass who could easily understand and relate to one another.

The lowest number of individuals (just 13 percent) were Collaborators. Collaborators are team-oriented and cooperative and fast trust builders in groups. With a relatively small sphere of influence in this group, Collaborators had their hands full trying to help these two teams to integrate. There were several individuals who had Collaborator as their second-strongest profile, so AchieveUnite brought this to their attention and offered them ways to build behaviors that would help them step up into this role when needed. This gave the Collaborators more power and influence in the group.

Sample Group

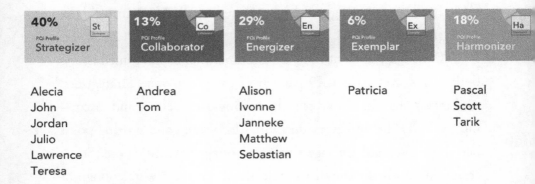

40% PQI Profile **Strategizer** St	13% PQI Profile **Collaborator** Co	29% PQI Profile **Energizer** En	6% PQI Profile **Exemplar** Ex	18% PQI Profile Harmonizer Ha
Alecia John Jordan Julio Lawrence Teresa	Andrea Tom	Alison Ivonne Janneke Matthew Sebastian	Patricia	Pascal Scott Tarik

As part of the experience, the group learned what individuals of each profile could offer in various scenarios. They began to see the possibilities for how they could work better together.

For example:

Exemplars who stand for ethical and honest behaviors could be useful as great mediators and excellent communicators during challenging situations. This would be a leadership competency that they could develop further and excel in.

Energizers understand how to bring out the best in others in an authentic and positive manner and love new initiatives. This is an important component for leading integrated teams during the early stages of working together.

Harmonizers have a high level of emotional intelligence and often present a calm demeanor to any situation. If they're kept appraised of changes and challenges, they can show up as a model for adapting to stress with composure.

What's important about this? In terms of change, each profile has predictable ways of responding and engaging. Once there was an awareness of each person's profile, open discussion ensued; and individuals from both teams began to acknowledge the resistance they were feeling. It was then possible to explore together how they could support each other to break through that resistance.

Results and ROI

The executive sponsor who had participated in all sessions said that she personally had gained a much deeper level of leadership confidence and competence that would be needed to lead this new integrated team.

Once the teams began to work more closely together, the executive sponsor estimated that they were at least six months ahead of all other similar teams in terms of productivity, sales, and, most of all, trust. They also experienced zero attrition during this time, an indicator of high employee engagement and satisfaction. Additionally, the individuals that participated in the AchieveUnite experience were taking what they had learned about building trusting relationships and applying it to their partnerships and customers, which was reaping measurable rewards.

In actuation: A study from KPMG found one in two M&As fail due to cultural differences. We cannot underestimate the impact of cultural integration on M&A success. It must be front and center; it must underpin every decision and become embedded within your business at every level.

"At Colt, we're integrating an exciting business we acquired to help us scale and grow," said Keri Gilder, CEO of Colt. "One of the first actions we took was to create a Culture Buddy program, to help our new combined community make friends and feel supported. More than 1,200 people participated, across regions, functions, and levels, and the feedback has been great. We're learning from each other, embracing our positive differences, and living one of our key values: to find a better way. It's a first step—and there is more to do—but it sends a clear message: 'We welcome you; we've got your back, and we're one business.'"

The PQi case study underscores the significance of trust and adaptability in a merger or acquisition. AchieveUnite's approach to resolving tensions between Companies A and B through tailored trust-building initiatives proved essential. The results highlight a crucial lesson for mergers and acquisitions: success hinges on addressing human dynamics as much as the strategic ones.

Craig Schlagbaum, former SVP of Channels at Comcast, thought about ways to leverage PQi to have different conversations with people depending on their trust-building style. Craig witnessed his team's excitement from their 2023 sales kickoff, where the team was introduced to PQi and participated in PQi workshops during their integration of Masergy and Comcast Business. Since he began using PQi for his team, he saw stronger collaboration, problem-solving, and communication, which translated into increased sales results and go-to-market efforts. Craig's skepticism of assessments turned to advocacy as he discovered the transformative impact of PQi on his team's performance and morale, proving that fine-tuning trust styles can unlock new realms of collaboration and achievement.

Sample PQi® Results Distribution

0%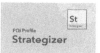

PQi Profile
Strategizer

Analytical, practical business advisor

Anup, Artur, Also, Anthony *, Carlos,
Denham, Edson, Fernando, Hani, Juan A*,
Juan C, Jonathan, Jay*, Marcel*, Nam*,
Netzer* RJ, Sergio, Thierry*

13%

PQi Profile
Collaborator

Empathetic, inclusive team builder

Nicole*, Benny, Ning, Pedro,
Pramod

3%

PQi Profile
Harmonizer

Emotionally intelligent, resilient mediator

Juan A*, Jay*, Marcel*, Daniel*,
Damian, Jean F, Jonathan S*,
Netzer*, Manuel, Pascal, Paul T

25%

PQi Profile
Exemplar

Principled, conscientious achiever

Anthony*, Daniel*, Nam*, Antonio,
Carole, Francois, Glenn, Jorge*, Moacyr,
Paul P, Richard, Thibault

29%

PQi Profile
Energizer

Positive, enthusiastic relationship builder

Jorge*, Jonathan S*, Thierry*,
Christian, Chia, Carl, George, Jeff
B, Kevin, Kirchiro, Marcelo,
Nicole*, Pat S

Here is an example of a company close to getting acquired at its worldwide sales meeting. The company had people from all over the world and with many experience levels. They realized from the PQi workshops how applicable trust-building styles are wherever in the world you are from. They saw they needed to bring more collaboration and collaborators to their meetings especially when they needed to have difficult conversations with each other or with partners. They also realized that 70 percent of the team had Strategizer as a dominant or second-dominant profile. And they needed to build their other "muscles" in Harmonizer, Exemplar, Collaborator, and Energizer! The company went on to get acquired and members of the team have said over and over how it helped them recognize how important partnering trust is and not everyone builds it the same way.

The Invaluable International Insights of PQi®

In international business, cultural nuances significantly impact collaboration and partnership success. The five profiles of the PQi Assessment—Strategizers, Energizers, Harmonizers, Collaborators, and Exemplars—often manifest differently across regions such as APAC, EMEA, and North America due to diverse business practices and cultural expectations.

Here is one example from work done with an international organization. Note the surprising differences between the business culture mindset of the regions.

By Region

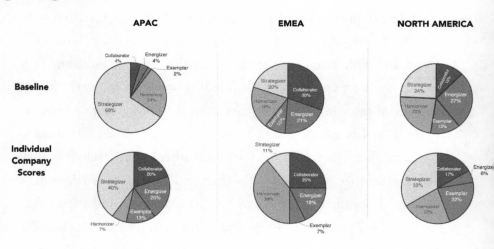

For instance, APAC business culture may place a high value on collective harmony and long-term relationships, which could result in a higher prevalence of Collaborators and Harmonizers. These profiles thrive in environments where teamwork and network building are essential. Understanding this can inform the approach to negotiations, partnerships, and team-building strategies in the APAC region.

In EMEA, which encompasses a wide range of cultures, there might be a balance between Strategizers, who emphasize data and logic, and Energizers and Exemplars, who focus on action and results. The diverse business environments from Western Europe's structured approach to the dynamic markets in the Middle East and Africa necessitate a nuanced understanding of how these profiles interact and influence business dealings.

North America, with a business environment that often rewards individual achievement and innovation, might see a higher representation of Energizers and Strategizers. These profiles resonate with the region's entrepreneurial spirit and a straightforward, results-oriented business approach.

In Latin America, the AchieveUnite team is still gathering more and more information. At the time of publication, we did not want to put North America and Latin America into the same region so are building an operating model in this region to also gather more trends and data.

By recognizing these regional tendencies, companies can tailor their international partnership strategies. For example, when partnering with APAC firms, it may be beneficial to emphasize team dynamics and long-term relationship building. In EMEA, demonstrating a balance between detailed strategic planning and the capability to execute efficiently can be key. Meanwhile, in North America, highlighting innovation and a strong track record of results may resonate more effectively.

Being able to appreciate the varying degrees of the five profiles across APAC, EMEA, North America, and Latin America is instrumental for international collaboration. It allows for the design of partnership approaches that align with regional business cultures, thereby fostering stronger, more effective international relationships.

The Power of the PQi®
Workshop Experience

Finishing the assessment is just the start of the journey to deploy your knowledge of your PQi profile to accelerate trust-building and improve your partnering relationships. The secret sauce of PQi is learning how to apply the concepts to yourself, your team, your organization, and your business partners adapting the tools in your partnering toolbox for the people and situation at hand. The workshop experiences offer a faster track to trusted relationships, partner alignment, and B2B success. These experiences, in turn, create measurable relationship results with your selected stakeholders, whether the partnering is:

- Internal in your own team

- Internal across functions

- Internal and external with your partners

- External with your partners and customers

- External with your industry influencers

- Internal with your board

- External with the partners you want to recruit

- External with your prospects

- External with your suppliers

- Your personal relationships

The benefits of these trusted relationships include access to proprietary information; a seat at the table to influence strategic decision-making; the opportunity to establish mutual, transformational success goals; and richer and deeper long-term satisfying trusted relationships.

Key Takeaways from Chapter 5

- Host a PQi Integration Workshop within the first month of merger proceedings to establish a common trust-building language, align disparate team cultures, and address integration challenges through guided dialogue and collaborative exercises.

- There are distinct differences in the prevalence of the PQi profiles across APAC, EMEA, and North America. These differences align with regional business practices and cultural expectations, which must be understood for successful international business collaborations.

- Understanding the dominant PQi profiles in each region can guide companies in customizing their partnership and negotiation strategies. For instance, emphasizing team dynamics in APAC, balancing strategy and execution in EMEA, and focusing on innovation and results in North America can lead to more effective international relationships.

- Recognizing how cultural nuances shape the PQi profiles and business interactions in different regions is crucial. Companies that account for these variations in their international strategies are likely to build stronger and more successful partnerships, as they can align their approaches with the local business culture.

Partnering Road Map—Action Steps

1. *Organizations should invest in training* their international business teams on the PQi profiles prevalent in their target regions. This training should focus on understanding the characteristics of Strategizers, Exemplars, Energizers, Collaborators, and Harmonizers within the context of the local business culture. This preparation will enable team members to recognize and adapt to the working styles and expectations they will encounter in different international markets.

2. *Create tailored frameworks for partnership strategies* that align with the predominant PQi profiles in each region. For APAC, this framework might emphasize collective harmony and long-term relationships; for EMEA, a balance between logical strategic planning and dynamic execution; and for North America, a focus on innovation and individual achievement. These frameworks should be flexible enough to accommodate the nuances within each region but structured enough to provide clear guidance on how to approach partnerships.

3. *Establish cultural liaison roles* within the organization to bridge the cultural and business practice gaps between regions. These liaisons would be responsible for keeping up-to-date with changes in local business cultures, advising on negotiation tactics, and helping teams navigate the complexities of international collaboration. By having dedicated personnel focused on understanding and communicating these cultural nuances, organizations can ensure that they are always approaching international relationships with the appropriate context and sensitivity.

CHAPTER 6

HARNESSING THE POWER OF A NORTH STAR STRATEGIC ALIGNMENT

The inception of any great partnership between two (or more) substantial entities begins with the alignment of vision. A shared vision acts as the Mission Statement, guiding all organizations involved toward a common future. A leader's role is to crystallize this vision, making it so compelling and clear that it resonates deeply within the organizations. When two large organizations share a vision and decide to embark on a journey together, the potential for impact is immense. The North Star Alignment is also applicable when large organizations are working with smaller organizations. In these scenarios, the alignment must be done at the sales and partner teams' level in the organization. However, this motion and joint vision alignment is a best practice for success. North Star Alignment is equally (if not more) important if there are three or more parties making up a solution, alliance, and/or new go-to-market. Harnessing the power of all and building strategic alignment becomes even more important and challenging.

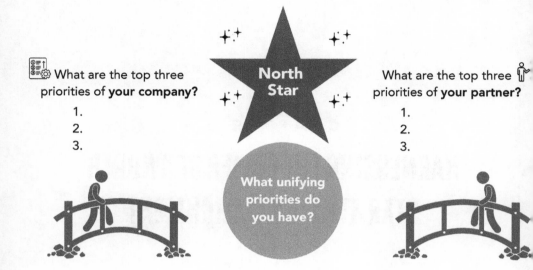

What are the top three priorities of **your company?**
1.
2.
3.

North Star

What unifying priorities do you have?

What are the top three priorities of **your partner?**
1.
2.
3.

Beyond the surface level of KPI alignment that was discussed in chapter 2 lies a more profound layer, which is termed "North Star" alignment. This involves the unification of mission and vision, steering the teams responsible for the relationship and those supporting it toward a common goal. This North Star Alignment transcends the tangibles and anchors itself in shared values and purposes. When done well the North Star serves as a foundation for the client's value as well.

This joint priority learning exercise sets the stage for establishing the Joint North Star, or taking on a Big Hairy Audacious Goal (BHAG). BHAG was first coined by Jim Collins in his book, *Good to Great*. Note, each company may have a BHAG—this alignment is around a joint BHAG and a Joint North Star! Jim Ritchings at AchieveUnite explains, "BHAGs have always meant to me 'stretch goal' or even beyond a stretch goal. A North Star is not necessarily a goal, it's a direction. So, aligning on both can be game changing for long-term business development growth."

*Anthony and Wendy were leaders representing two partner-
ing organizations. As they sat down, with the COVID scare
lifting, they wondered what it would take to light a common
and unifying fire under their respective teams. What was needed
to affect a needed culture change? Each of their respective organizations had recently gone through a restructuring to make the
challenge even more daunting.*

*Anthony and Wendy agreed that they needed to create a unified
enthusiasm around big joint challenges. The joint BHAG goal
established was 350 new partners jointly selling and active with
the two companies in twelve months. During the revenue acceleration program, they asked their teams, working together, to
create innovative joint plans that would stimulate new thinking
and excite commitment. The teams then implemented the most
creative ideas. It was a definite revenue accelerator, according
to Anthony and Wendy as they reviewed the successes, post-
program. BHAGs are uniters and vision creators. They inspire
and motivate the teams. When successfully achieved, BHAGs
set the stage for more aggressive goals and celebrations down
the road. BHAG "planning and brainstorming" also sets the
stage for partnering teams to innovate, for teams to create new
business models, opportunities, or programs. These are the kinds
of programs where magic gets created when done well!*

"Companies who are most successful with their channel
initiatives and partnerships have an opportunity to increase
internal collaboration as well to fuel productivity and growth.
North Star Alignment can be used for this initiative as well."

–ACHIEVEUNITE'S PARTNER LIFETIME VALUE EBOOK

For a partnership to thrive, there must be a cultural cohesion that transcends organizational boundaries. This involves recognizing the unique cultural elements of each organization and finding common ground where a shared identity can be fostered.

The essence of a partnership between two or more organizations lies in leveraging each other's strengths. As CEOs and leaders, it's essential to identify and capitalize on these synergies. It could be a combination of technological capabilities, market reach, or research and development prowess.

Here are sample questions to ask during your strategic planning workshops to uncover:

- *How do you differentiate with customers?*

- *What is your unique value?*

- *What are your top priority areas for growth in the next twelve months?*

- *What internal metrics do you use and in what cadence to capture the health of your company?*

It's important that you bring these answers clearly to your joint planning sessions as well.

Samples of compelling joint value propositions could be:

1. Build new joint business in a vertical market, an industry, a region, or a segment.

2. Build a new joint solution that is unique.

3. Build a joint solution that is disruptive to a loyal base with a compelling ROI.

4. Build a joint service offering that is compelling for a set of customers.

Joint North Star Value Propositions

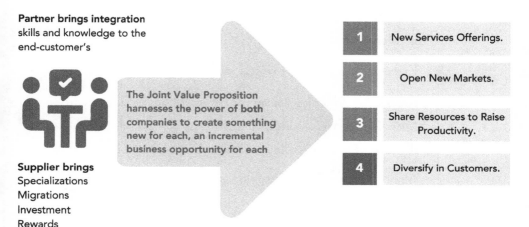

Partner brings integration skills and knowledge to the end-customer's

The Joint Value Proposition harnesses the power of both companies to create something new for each, an incremental business opportunity for each

Supplier brings
Specializations
Migrations
Investment
Rewards

1	New Services Offerings.
2	Open New Markets.
3	Share Resources to Raise Productivity.
4	Diversify in Customers.

But how do you identify these?

Two ways to get to your joint value proposition are to conduct North Star Workshops and Partnering Success Experiences together with your partner like the Anthony and Wendy example. Build a joint SWOT analysis of your partnership and then build a joint value proposition to the specific target customers or markets.

Another way to build this is to leverage our interactive brainstorming workshops to build your joint value proposition.

To conduct your own Joint North Star workshop, answer the following seven questions:

1. What are the top priorities for this partnership?

2. What are the top priorities of each of us?

3. What one priority can we both establish that will hit both of our goals?

4. What value does each party (partner/supplier) bring to this priority?

   Note: More and detailed and specific value elements are critical: vertical market, resources, services, reporting, AI enablement.

5. Then, what is a picture of success for a customer?

6. What value do they get from the benefit of our value elements? *Note:* if you have a value that any of the companies individually cannot deliver to the customer, you are on the right track.

7. What challenges and impact does this value proposition solve for the customer?

For example, let's say this unique joint saves them six months of labor, it saves them resources, it saves them hard dollars, maybe they can offer a new product to their customers. The more impact and more hard-dollar value elements, the better to create stickiness and a more compelling joint value (NORTH STAR) proposition.

Here are two very different examples of organizations who do partnering well and whose value with partners has achieved the 10× factor:

Hewlett Packard Inc. is one of the staple companies in American history and a strong global brand. The company, over many years, has built a global network of partners operating in more than 170 countries. MaryBeth Walker, an industry expert in partnering at HP, shared this story:

At HP, channel partners are part of our DNA. Since the company was formed eighty years ago our strategy has been to have channel partners embedded into our go-to-market strategy. We consider them part of our sales force and give them the same training and sales assets we make available to our direct sales reps. When the need arises to invest in our partner programs and associated channel infrastructure, our executive staff doesn't have to be convinced of the value the channel brings. It is a given that any such investments are business critical. Our channel ecosystem is fundamental to our success, and I don't have to convince anyone of the value.

Denise Hayman was the chief revenue officer at Expel, a security operations provider. She asked AchieveUnite to help her accelerate the revenue growth with Expel's partner network. Through this engagement, Denise and her sales team learned the following:

1. Which partners fit Expel's value proposition best.

2. What their ideal partners wanted from Expel to grow.

3. What their competition was doing to create stronger partner loyalty.

4. What they could do that would be a unique benefit for the partner.

5. How they would build partnerships at scale to help the small team of partner managers accelerate incremental revenue.

The team built and executed a very targeted plan that benefited those partners' businesses and within two years the partner business grew from 0 to 35 percent of Expel's revenue and was the fastest portion of their growth. The partners who worked with Expel developed new service offerings and Expel had new markets to penetrate.

Loyal, lifetime value partnerships are the way of the future. After eight years of working with clients in strategy and execution, evidence now shows that CEOs, CROs, and corporate boards who figure this out and properly build partnerships into their organization's DNA will be the most successful over this next decade, because things are changing so fast and there are new ways to buy and new technology like artificial intelligence disrupting everything. For businesses to do well, leaders and workers all need to know how to work well with customers, partners, employees, and suppliers and be more creative and agile than in the past.

Think about how good partnering helps each of these scenarios:

- *Speed is critical*—Today's digital and social world mandates solutions within days, weeks, and months. People are no longer willing to wait years.

- *Flexibility is essential*—You want choices in how and what you consume. Another reason partners who can give this flexibility and guarantees are essential.

- *Organizations need to anticipate changing customer needs*— New kinds of expertise across a customer's journey help keep them engaged and loyal.

- *True solutions are now often from more than one company*— Companies design solutions from multiple areas: think hospitals in healthcare, managed services providers in tech, accounting firms in finance, airlines in transportation.

- *Companies need to expand their reach*—new customers, new geographies, new vertical markets, new segment size of customers. Think product manufacturers, pharmaceutical makers, and technology vendors—all partner with companies who can expand their solutions to reach the customer base in different geographies, verticals, embedded into solutions.

- *Hybrid and remote employees are challenged with connectedness, communication, productivity, and balance*—They need to be connected and partnered with remote colleagues to make things work.

- *Increasing productivity in the workplace is essential for organizational success*—Work environment and work cultures are two of the top factors affecting employees' productivity in the workplace.

At the heart of these endeavors is the unwavering commitment to forge a partnership that capitalizes on combined strengths and strives toward shared objectives. The underlying principle is straightforward: by synergizing efforts, organizations can achieve breakthroughs in innovation, expand their market reach, and enhance operational efficiency—creating a partnership that is indeed more impactful than the individual contributions.

Adopting this comprehensive strategy enables large-scale entities to establish "North Star" alliances that propel not just short-term aims but also pave the way for enduring leadership and market transformation. For CEOs and key decision-makers, this represents the avenue to strategic partnerships that possess the potential to reshape the future trajectory of their enterprises.

Key Takeaways from Chapter 6

- At the heart of every effective partnership between large organizations is a shared vision, or a North Star Alignment. This shared vision guides every level of the organization, from the executive team to the remote worker, ensuring that everyone is moving cohesively toward the same overarching goal. This is especially true of two large organizations; however, the same North Star Alignment is essential for any type of partnership—the onus for those may fall on the region or the vertical.

- For your partnerships to truly thrive, there must be a cultural cohesion that goes beyond the boundaries of each organization. Identifying and capitalizing on each other's strengths, such as technological capabilities, market reach, and R&D expertise, is essential for creating a strong and productive joint value proposition.

- Your organization must utilize a variety of strategic methods to form partnerships including industry events and associations, professional matchmaking companies, digital platforms specific to industry, and business development outreach. Establishing a robust joint value proposition that follows your North Star mission is crucial for the short- and long-term success of any partnership. This joint value proposition helps to focus everyone's effort on the right things for navigating the complexities of a partnership and driving success.

Partnering Road Map–Action Steps

1. *Develop a Joint North Star Vision Statement.* Collaborate with your potential partner(s) to create a clear and compelling joint vision statement. This statement should resonate with both organizations and act as a guiding North Star for all strategic decisions and actions within the partnership.

2. *Create a Joint North Start Value Proposition Framework.* The joint value proposition that can be marketed on a one pager and can be put into a pitch deck for a customer or prospect. Use a joint SWOT workshop to help get the best ideas from the key members out on the table.

3. *Foster Strong Cultural Integration* and ensure the right structured KPIs, governance, and cadence are discussed and agreed upon. (Refer to chapter 2 for specifics.)

You must begin to actively work toward creating a cohesive culture between the partnering organizations. Identify and celebrate the unique cultural elements of each organization and find common values to create a shared identity. Build a detailed "partnership alliance architecture" by establishing joint governance structures, aligning resources, and setting up shared processes and communication protocols. This infrastructure is essential for managing your partnership effectively and should be designed to handle the complexities and scale of the collaboration.

CHAPTER 7

ACHIEVING YOUR "PARTNERING GROWTH DNA"

DEEPENING TRUST AND RELATIONSHIP AS THE CATALYST FOR GROWTH AND PRODUCTIVITY

Strategic partnerships are applicable in every industry in the world, and their successful execution yields remarkable advantages. As discussed in chapter 2, companies ingrained with a "Partnering Growth DNA" showcase an incredible surge in productivity—up to 50 percent more according to a study conducted in collaboration with the University of Glasgow, focused on Partner Life Time Value. Such organizations don't just benefit from heightened productivity; they also enjoy heightened employee engagement, innovation, and a collective drive toward success. Our eight-year journey involving thousands of global interviews revealed a solid insight: Embarking on the journey of relationship development is pivotal for any professional aiming to excel in the realm of partnerships. This section is designed to guide you through the nuances of cultivating trusted relationships that intertwine personal rapport with business acumen, transforming you into an indispensable business advisor.

"A company's reputation, its ability to partner and collaborate with others, its capacity to innovate, its effectiveness in engaging its people, its ability to attract and retain good people, the speed at which it can execute—all these dimensions of success, plus many more, are powerfully affected by trust."

—STEPHEN R. COVEY

Let's explore the Partnering Growth DNA: once a unified vision or North Star is defined, the focus shifts to constructing the partnership infrastructure. This "alliance architecture" is about putting in place joint governance mechanisms, aligning resources, and defining common processes and communication standards. Such a structure is essential for managing the intricacies that come with scaling a partnership and will be discussed in detail in Part 3 of our discussion.

Scale Trust Across Multiple Partnerships

In a business environment where your organization is cultivating multiple partnerships and customer relationships simultaneously, the principles of trust must be scaled without diluting their potency. Here's how to amplify the Partnering Growth DNA across various collaborations effectively:

1. *Standardize Trust-Building Frameworks:* Develop a consistent trust-building framework that can be applied across all partnerships. This should include standardized practices for transparency, communication, and mutual goal setting. A uniform approach ensures that each partner and customer receives the same level of commitment and clarity from your organization.

2. *Personalize Interactions within the Framework:* While the framework for building trust remains consistent, the interactions within it should be personalized. Tailor your approach to the unique needs and cultures of each partner or customer, demonstrating that your commitment to the relationship is as unique as they are.

> *"Trust is the glue of life. It's the foundational principle that holds all relationships."*
> **–STEPHEN R. COVEY**

Imagine a world where every business interaction is underpinned by unshakable trust. In this chapter, let's delve further into the critical dimension of the system for partnering success: Relationship Development. Fostering trust-based relationships that lead to business success but transform you into a sought-after business advisor in today's collaborative business landscape.

3. *Empower Teams with Trust-Building Autonomy:* Train and empower your teams to make decisions that reinforce trust-building within partnerships. When teams are skilled in the art of trust and given the autonomy to act, they can adapt to the nuances of each relationship, fostering a deep sense of reliability and commitment.

4. *Leverage Technology for Consistency and Transparency:* Utilize technology platforms that facilitate consistent and transparent communication across all partnerships. Tools that provide clear visibility into project statuses, performance metrics, and strategic objectives help maintain a foundation of trust.

5. *Monitor and Measure Relationship Health:* Establish metrics to regularly assess the health of each relationship. Use tools like Net Promoter Scores (NPSs), regular feedback sessions, and relationship audits to gauge trust levels and identify areas for improvement.

6. *Celebrate Shared Successes Publicly:* Recognize and celebrate successes and milestones achieved through partnerships. Public acknowledgment of collaborative achievements reinforces trust and showcases the value of the relationship to all stakeholders involved.

7. *Conduct Regular Strategic Reviews:* Hold periodic strategic reviews with partners to realign on goals, evaluate the progress of the relationship, and adjust, as necessary. These reviews should be collaborative and focused on continuous improvement.

By implementing these steps, organizations can ensure that the Partnering Growth DNA, with trust at its core, is not only preserved but strengthened as you or your organization expands the network of partnerships and customer engagements. This approach transforms companies into trusted advisors and preferred partners in respective industries.

Case Study: The ConnectWise Trust Paradigm

Let's look at ConnectWise. Mike Goldberg, VP of Sales at ConnectWise, leverages trust as a core business strategy. This case study illustrates the tangible benefits of trust in customer relationships and business growth.

Mike Goldberg, head of sales at ConnectWise, a provider of platform systems to over thirty thousand technology services providers worldwide, understands Partnering Growth DNA. ConnectWise's clients are technology solution providers providing product and services support to hundreds of thousands of small and medium-sized businesses. Mike's mission is centered on partner success: "To empower IT solution providers with unmatched software, services, and community to achieve their most ambitious vision of success." Mike is also an authority and long-time sales and partnering executive to small businesses.

ConnectWise provides the nervous systems that their partners use to run their businesses reliably. Mike explains the priorities in his role as head of sales: "At ConnectWise, we must first establish a level of trust that opens doors to partnering possibilities. After which, our every action we take, combined with our product and service reliability must reinforce and grow the level of trust. At our base, we are trust providers."

Mike talks about executive to client trust as the foundation and then the trust and success happen as people align on top-line goals, bottom-line goals, operational practices, and long-term vision. The stickiness and loyalty happen from that joint alignment and success. Trust is an emotion first and then deepened and continued with strategic value.

By aligning top-line and bottom-line goals, operational practices, and long-term vision, ConnectWise fosters loyalty and trust that translate into sustainable business success. This approach is essential to creating the trust-building and strategic value alignment needed in organizations.

You learned about PQi® profiles and how individuals interact to build trust. But it does not stop there. Just as individuals have profiles, so do teams and organizations. These group profiles are often referred to as cultures or DNAs. Functions often have distinct cultures within the organization. Their purpose and their metrics may be in conflict. For example, the purchasing department may be focused on inventory turnover, finance focused on return on equity, and sales focused on revenue targets. Individually, these measures are important for any business. The conflicts will be evident to insiders and outsiders alike unless the president, CEO, and/or board establish a hierarchy of values and DNA priorities.

Organizations have a culture as they interact with partner organizations. PQi also provides a bridge to understand and mesh these different DNAs. When working with other organizations, it's crucial that everyone shares the same values and goals for success. Without open conversations and a collective understanding, it's tough for everyone involved to make the best choices where their business interests and priorities meet.

That is why organizations and teams need to know their own PQi strengths, and their priorities and how those priorities line up to the North Star. Also, it is important to know the PQi profiles of the CEO and CFO of the organization you're dealing with. It's a code that unlocks effective communication. Mastering this skill will empower you to influence and connect better with partner organizations.

Once you are fluent in the PQi language and can spot it in others, your interactions will become much more insightful, valuable, and productive.

Here are ten partnering trust tips to accelerate trust with any PQi profile. *Check the ones you feel you are already strong with, and X the ones that you may want to improve. This checklist will serve as an excellent foundation for your own personal development plan as it relates to the famous soft skills required in this next era for success.*

- *Lean into difficult conversations.* It's important to lean into these tough situations or areas where you sense disagreement. People deepen trust through sharing and conquering challenges. See the Difficult Conversations Template on page 100 to leverage as a tool for improving your skills in this domain.

- *Plan trust-building experiences.* This could be a PQi workshop, a sporting event, or a fun get-together. Julianne Zuber, tech industry executive and US federal market expert, always says, "It's important to leverage opportunities to conduct modern-day trust falls. PQi experiences can be perfect for this purpose."

- *Pay attention to cultural differences.* As discussed in the previous chapter, whether North America, Europe, Africa, Asia, or Latin America, cultural differences are everywhere, and within geographies, differences, while more subtle, abound. Apply time and energy to understand them and show others you care, and your partners will respect you more and lay out their version of a red carpet.

- *Offer genuine acknowledgment or validation.* Acknowledging your partner's strengths and referencing their successes—big or small—show that you are paying attention to small and large accomplishments.

- *Remain calm in difficult situations.* Your poise and steadiness are contagious. When you're aware of your emotional triggers and manage your emotions, you model how to handle difficult situations. Your partners will also become calmer and have greater confidence in you.

- *Take time to care and be vulnerable.* Admitting that you don't have all the answers demonstrates honesty, which is critical to building trust. It also encourages others to step up to lead or solve problems. Take the time to care and ask and learn about others. This genuine concern for others' well-being is a key element of partnering trust.

- *Follow through on your promises.* Integrity is an essential element of trust. When you say what you'll do and do what you say consistently, trust grows. Make any commitments visible to your partner and follow through with them immediately. The mantra of Jeff Spalding, Spalding Solutions' president, is "Always provide Value—give more than you receive as part of all you do."

- *Give credit where credit is due.* Clearly, none of us can be successful in a vacuum. When you empower others to have the spotlight, it also shines on you like a guiding light. This recognition builds trust and a sense of goodwill within a team.

- *Act on behalf of the "common good".* Benevolence, the willingness to put others before yourself, is not often seen as a business imperative. Yet, you likely see repeatedly that the people who practice this are among the most trusted individuals in any company.

- *Continue working on your Partnering Trust Growth Mindset.* Partnering Growth and Resilience lead to growth actions, growth actions lead to growth relationships, growth relationships lead to personal and business growth. You shape your universe through every single interaction you have, and the choices you make. See the Resilience part of this chapter for specifics on how to foster your Partnering Trust Growth Mindset.

Partnering trust is earned in drops and lost in buckets. Think about a time in your life when you lost trust in someone, or when they broke their trust in you. It only takes one incident to destroy the years of trust that have been earned.

Let's look at an example:

A leader of a sales team promised the team they would receive a performance bonus if they achieved a specific goal by the end of the quarter. Members of the team worked hard to achieve the goal; however, when the time came to distribute the bonuses, they were told that the money was just not there. The team was deflated and trust in their leader was diminished. The leader's credibility was now on the line, and without proper action on his part it is quite possible that his words would always be questioned in the future.

So, what do you do if the trust you have earned has been breached? While trust is not easy to repair once it has been broken, there are steps that can be taken and should be taken as soon as possible. Mending a fractured relationship calls for having a sincere and courageous conversation.

When a promise has been broken, as it was in the scenario above, you must take ownership of what has happened and acknowledge the impact this has had on others. It is important to not defend actions—but rather to be clear that you should have behaved in a different manner. You must allow time for those who have been impacted to feel their emotions—even if they are negatively directed toward you. Ask the team what they need from you to regain their trust. Next, you must verbalize a commitment to new behavior in the future and then put words into consistent action.

Restoring trust when it has been broken in business is not easy. But by having honest conversations, taking new actions consistently, and then having patience, trust can be restored and sustained in the future.

The sales leader brought everyone together and made a commitment that he would share the profits of the team when collectively they brought the numbers up. He was transparent with the numbers, and together they worked to achieve the profit pool so they all could receive their bonus. Together they increased the business and the core team who cared about the mission stayed and helped the group through the tough times.

Having difficult conversations is critical for trust-building. *Here are tips to see how well you are managing yourself through difficult conversations:*

Have the Difficult Conversations= Change the Game Conversations

1. Set the right mindset	2. Set the rules of engagement	3. Clearly state the purpose of the conversation	4. Stay calm and centered	5. Plan the conversation but don't script
6. Keep an open mind	7. Make an agreement to listen	8. Clarify what you heard	9. Seek input on problem solving	10. Slow down the conversation if necessary

Difficult Conversations Template (visit https://www.achieveunite.com/ partneringsuccessbookresources/ to download the template)

Three Phases of Difficult Conversations

Preparation Phase

Give yourself time to plan out what you want to say. The more thought you give prior to the conversation the more likely there will be a positive outcome. Take time to self-reflect on your motives. Some people enter a conversation, often not even being aware of wanting to prove they are right and defend their actions. These mindsets are rarely productive.

As the initiator of the conversation, you want to think of your most desired outcomes. Do you want to make amends? Are you committed to a change in behavior? Do you have any requests of the other person? Take time to consider the other person's perspective and any impact you may have had on them. You also want to note your own current emotional state and plan to put a check on any unhelpful emotions.

It is also wise to consider the other person's responses and/or any challenges that could emerge during the conversation. The more you plan for these the better prepared you will be. Once you have thoroughly considered the situation you will be ready to enter the second phase of the actual conversation with greater clarity.

Having the Conversation

The foundation for all productive conversations, especially when trust has been broken, is to actively listen and to ask questions that help uncover what the other person is feeling. This is where you will need to control your own strong emotions, be curious about what the other person has to say, and be humble enough to hear and empathize with their point of view.

It is important to take ownership of what has happened and to acknowledge the impact this has had on the other person. It is important not to defend your actions—but rather to be clear that you should have behaved in a different manner. You must allow those who have been impacted time to feel their emotions—even if they are negatively directed toward you. Ask them what they need from you to regain their trust. Next, you must verbalize a commitment to new behavior in the future, then you must put your words into consistent action.

Post-Conversation: Follow Through

The final phase of constructive conversation is the follow-through. You could have had a very productive conversation, but all your work will be in vain if you fail to follow through. Develop a plan for yourself that includes new actions and new behaviors. Communicate this plan to the other party and set regular check-ins to determine how each of you is feeling about the attempts for repair.

Restoring trust when it has been broken in business is not easy. But with thoughtful planning, skillful conversations, taking new actions consistently, and then having patience, trust can be restored and sustained in the future.

Additional Partnering Tip: Cultivating Your Own Resilience and Growth Partnering Mindset

Carmen Sorice, an AchieveUnite and Partnering expert, is passionate about resilience. He has had situations including the loss of a son that forced him to exercise resilience. "We are all experiencing perpetual change, and the pace of change is accelerating. This change is continuously testing our human ability to adapt, survive, and thrive.

This requires us to embrace a positive mentality to build the skills to adapt to changing conditions and have the knowledge of how to build trust with our customers, partners, and industry colleagues, and to be RESILIENT. This is especially true in the partnering world. As a channel chief for twenty years, I have always sought to hire professionals with 'thick skin.'"

As a pro, you get hit from many sides. On the partner front, you must deal with your partners' challenges, which include channel conflicts, margin pressure, and enablement. Internally you must battle with Sales, Finance, Marketing, Pricing, Customer Service, Professional Services, and the endless pursuit to prove WHY it is critical to work with partners. In addition to managing through the typical sales and operational challenges, partnering pros also need to deal with unique partner-related challenges and conflicts. Did the partner violate trust? Did the direct sales team "go around" the partner? Did one partner try to squeeze out another partner? Did a renewals specialist try to renew a contract direct, after a partner had been servicing the customer?

Managing through this partner conflict requires thick skin. It requires resilience and a growth mindset. Many people think you either have resilience or you don't. However, at AchieveUnite, we believe that these skills are developed with a concrete focus, practice, and experience. And building your resilience and growth mindset will lead to higher qualities of life, and higher levels of trust-building and long-term partnerships. Here is a checklist to help you cultivate your partnering trust growth mindset and resilience:

			Checklist – Actions to build your growth mindset and resilience
Mentality	Develop and sustain a positive mentality. Be the victor, not the victim. CHOOSE to be positive. Attitude is a choice!	1	Check your attitude early in the day. Do an honest assessment. Adjust, as necessary.
		2	Subscribe to daily inspirational quotes. Read, read again, read more.
Adaptability	Learn to be comfortable, being UN-comfortable. Develop the knowledge and skills necessary to keep moving forward.	3	Identify the skills required for continued growth in your life, and in your industry.
		4	1 percent rule: Improve your knowledge and skills by 1 percent each day. The compound effect is exponential.
Trust	Leverage a set of trustworthy relationships. Consciously build and enhance trust with key relationships.	5	Deepen Trust: Proactively engage and reengage with people and partners you trust.
		6	Build Trust: Understand how you and others build trust. Adjust your approach.

Remember, every interaction is an opportunity to either build or erode trust. The journey is challenging but incredibly rewarding.

Key Takeaways from Chapter 7

- Trust as a Foundational Business Strategy: Mike Goldberg emphasizes the critical importance of establishing trust as a foundation for successful partnerships. At ConnectWise, building a level of trust that enables new partnering possibilities is considered a primary objective.

- Evaluate the Role of Strategic Positioning in Partnership: Mike Goldberg's mission at ConnectWise to empower IT solution providers underscores the necessity of strategic positioning within the industry. The concept of having a "seat at the table" is not just about participation but about influencing the direction and success of partnerships.

- Evaluate the Ten Skills for Trust-Building and Pick One or Two Areas to Improve You and Your Team's Skills: The approach at ConnectWise involves aligning top-line and bottom-line goals, operational practices, and long-term vision to create partnership stickiness and loyalty.

Partnering Road Map–Action Steps

1. *Implement a Standardized Trust-Building Protocol.* Create and apply a set of consistent trust-building practices across all partnerships, such as transparent communication, shared goal setting, and regular feedback mechanisms.

2. *Personalize Your Partnership Approach.* Tailor your engagement strategies to the specific needs and cultural nuances of each partner, demonstrating that your investment in the relationship is as individualized as the partner itself.

3. *Empower and Train Your Team.* Equip your team with the skills and authority to foster trust in their interactions with partners, ensuring that they can adapt these principles to the unique dynamics of each relationship.

PART 3

BUSINESS ACCELERATION

CHAPTER 8

IDENTIFYING AND ALIGNING THE FIVE "P"s FOR GROWTH

In this section, let's look at the second dimension of successful partnering: the Business Accelerator. True value-based partnering in the B2B world requires a win-win recipe for success. The more interdependent the businesses are, the greater the opportunity for a strategic relationship and higher success and growth rates. To navigate the complexities of partnering success, you are introduced to the Five "P"s of Partnering—a comprehensive model that addresses the Business Acceleration facets of partnership dynamics, ensuring a robust and synergistic partnering ecosystem of influence and value.

The following case study shows how Bill, a former Air Force avionics mechanic, applied his military technical skills to revolutionize his family's traditional irrigation business, Water Meters Inc. (WMI), amid the challenging drought conditions of California's Central Valley. His strategic vision for WMI harnessed the power of emerging technologies and strong personal relationships to drive the company's growth into new markets and collaborative partnerships.

After completing his electronics curriculum at a community college, Bill joined the Air Force hoping for adventure, and landed a role as an avionics mechanic in Alaska. Upon completing his tour, he returned to help with the family business, Water Meters Inc., a distributor of irrigation systems in California's Central Valley. Bill's Air Force experience, particularly in teamwork and technical skills, unexpectedly prepared him to lead WMI into the world of partnerships. He also saw changes coming to both the supply and demand partner segments.

With strong relationships established with suppliers and clients, Bill recognized impending changes in the irrigation industry. New suppliers were introducing wireless technology and sensors, mirroring his experience with aircraft systems. Additionally, clients faced challenges due to California's drought conditions, prompting Bill to consider expanding WMI's market to adjacent sectors such as golf courses, college campuses, and corporate complexes, as well as neighboring states like Nevada and Arizona.

Seeing an opportunity for growth, Bill aimed to leverage his personal connections to benefit suppliers, clients, and WMI. He sought to move beyond being seen as just a trusted friend to becoming a strategic partner, envisioning a leadership role in partner decision-making processes.

Bill's strategy involved gaining a "seat at the table" with key partners, allowing him to influence their business strategies and contribute to their success. This initiative required a shift in cultural leadership, with Bill aiming to catalyze this change and establish himself as a vital player in the partner ecosystem. By embracing innovation and strategic thinking, Bill aimed to propel WMI into new markets and solidify its position as a leader in the irrigation industry.

In many situations, a major cultural leadership change initiative will be necessary. In Bill's case, he felt he could be the catalyst. To do so, he needed to have a "seat at the table" with the selected partners. For now, let's say that a Seat at the Partner's Table allows you to influence the partners' business strategy and help deliver success, and this is SUCCESS AS defined by the partner. The table refers to the location where the partner's decision-makers meet to make resource allocations, set business priorities, and consider financing alternatives. It might be a real table, for example, in a Board of Directors conference room. Or it might be at an offsite venue, or a virtual table in a video planning session.

The Five "P"s of Partnering

In an increasingly interconnected business world, the art of forging and nurturing partnerships is more critical than ever. The Business Accelerator framework recognizes this and offers a structured approach to optimize and systematize such collaborations. To navigate the complexities of partnering, here is a comprehensive model that addresses the major facets of partnership dynamics, ensuring a growth structure and model for success.

These five P components are designed to guide leaders and organizations in:

- creating effective partnerships and structures aligned with the organization's core values and operational strategies

- leverage the strengths of their people

- recognize the unique value of each partner

- streamline processes for mutual benefit

- cocreate actionable plans for joint success

Each "P" invites introspective and strategic questions that serve as a road map for evaluating and enhancing the partnership journey, making the five "P"s an indispensable tool for any partnership leader aiming for growth and excellence.

The Five "P"s for the Business Accelerator Initiatives

Five "P"s of Partnering

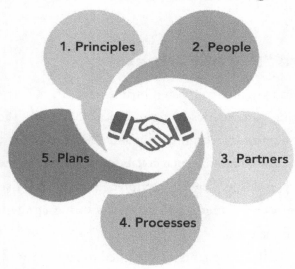

The five partnering "P"s:

1. The *Principles* of your organization as they apply to partners.

   a. Do your North Star Guiding Principles identify your partnering values?

   b. Do your partners know what you stand for?

    c. Are all functions of your organization committed to partner success?

    d. How does your organization best align with your partner organizations?

    e. Do you have a Partner LifeTime Value® mindset?

2. The *People* across your organization, especially those working directly with partners.

    a. Who will lead (or leads) the partnering initiative? What one person is ultimately responsible for the success?

    b. Who are the key executives also aligned and accountable for success?

    c. Is accountability established and visible?

    d. What is the hiring profile for our people that provide the front line for partners?

    e. What personalities, competencies, and skills do we select and teach our partner-facing resources?

3. The *Partners* you recruit and nurture. All partners are not equal. Companies put in place all sorts of processes to standardize the partner experience and the transactions. It's equally important to understand and jointly build unique value with your partners:

    a. Do we have methods to recognize and acknowledge the uniqueness of each partner?

    b. Who is our ideal partner? What does the profile look like?

    c. How do partners build their unique value to their clients with us?

4. The *Processes* you implement with partners.

   a. What are the platforms you are implementing to assist the partner in doing business in general, and specifically with your company?

   b. Is your organization's automation simple for the partner to implement and leverage for its benefit?

   c. Are the business practices you have relating to partners straightforward?

5. The *Plan*: A Joint Plan with your partner (partners) is your joint success playbook.

   a. Do you have a planning process for each strategic partner that produces a set of joint commitments?

   b. Do you plan on your calendar, theirs, or both? For example, our company finished the fiscal year in October; the partner, in December. So let's agree to do six planning sessions with execs at the July mark to ensure you hit both planning cycles.

   c. Does the plan generate a series of joint investments designed to grow both organizations' businesses?

   d. Is each partner's plan customized for the maturity of the relationship?

   e. Are the plans simple, actionable, and valuable for both organizations?

Case Study in Action:

An example of a company doing this well is Atlassian. Ko Mistry, VP Global Partnerships, describes software company Atlassian's journey to a Partnering Growth DNA company:

> *"At the beginning, when we began to lay out our go-to-market game plan, one of our strategies was to build a product that was easy to purchase and easy to consume—and one that would create a community around it. This community would affect how the product was bought, used, and supported, leading to a viral, self-supporting system. This flywheel effect led to the product becoming more and more viral."*

Atlassian made two pivotal decisions very early on that led to partners becoming the core of their go-to-market strategy:

- *They initially decided not to invest in salespeople because of the viral nature of how the product was getting adopted and utilized. Later, as they matured, investment in sales teams became an imperative and their sellers are brilliant at the co-sell motion according to partners who have built a significant practice with Atlassian.*

- *They decided not to become a services company early in the company journey—instead to stay a SaaS because directly providing services could conflict with their partner business proposition. This they did not want to do. Instead, their partners could build their own intellectual property, applications, and services around Atlassian solutions.*

Atlassian knew their target market and realized that partners were a strong route to market. These two decisions led to partners developing their business solutions around Atlassian products. Groups of individuals created partnerships with Atlassian because of the business opportunity that it posed. As enterprise customers started to deploy Atlassian products across their entire organization, Atlassian offered partners a fantastic business opportunity to be those experts, help them integrate and utilize the products, adoption, training, etc.

Because Atlassian started as a partner-first company, partners are ingrained across all components of Atlassian's customer-facing models. As Ko says: "Partnering is a core part of our DNA—when we attend trade shows—it's important that we have our partners there. This is a win-win. It helps us scale from a marketing standpoint. Our partners have helped us reach more than two hundred countries. Now, if you take that to all the go-to-market functions, we will be able to accelerate both marketing and sales. We leveraged our partners to help us reach more than 250,000 paying customers, which has been an incredible business model for our partners as well as Atlassian.

"When you think about what a solution partner can do with Atlassian—take the core product, add some components of their own services, as well as marketplace apps—suddenly, you've got a customer solution to take to market. So, the extensibility and use cases around the platform become so large," says Mistry.

"Atlassian's mentality that partners are an extension of them has led to an ideal business value proposition. How to work with partners is ingrained across the entire organization," adds Mistry.

The Atlassian story is unique and has much in common with some of the other stories in this book: partners and the complementary ecosystem go hand in hand. For Atlassian, the technology ecosystem is part of that original notion of building tools that are easy to adopt. They built a mechanism where other companies can create applications and values to extend the functionality of the core product. That translates into more than 1,500 partners building tools that enhance Atlassian's overall value to different customers, vertical industries, and geographies, creating a whole world of different use cases and examples. This part of the System for Partnering Success looks at the strength of B2B connection between the respective partners. In other words, how do you leverage the elements of Business Accelerator and interdependence between/among partners?

Atlassian is a terrific case study. The Business Accelerator is a pivotal dimension in the realm of strategic partnering. Bill's story, with his transition from the Air Force to leading WMI, exemplifies the power of leveraging personal relationships and technical acumen to propel a family business into the future through innovative partnerships. It's a narrative that resonates with the transformative journey of Atlassian, where strategic decisions to prioritize a partner-first approach unlocked global reach and extraordinary growth.

From having a seat at the decision-making table to embracing a Partnering DNA culture, the principles outlined here are universal. They apply not only to giant and midsize companies in this book but to any organization, regardless of size or industry, looking to accelerate their business. Strategic partnering is an accelerator with so many culture benefits associated with this growth strategy.

The journey through the Business Accelerator dimension reveals that when you focus and build your strategy around the five Ps, you set the stage for a mutual ascent to new heights of achievement and innovation.

The motions of partner collaboration can be automated to allow more personal time and energy in developing the strategic partnering connection.

-Frie Pétré,
Founder & CEO, Qollabi

Key Takeaways from Chapter 8

- Success in B2B partnerships is rooted in interdependence; the closer the collaboration, the greater the shared success. This approach elevates partnerships beyond mere transactions to strategic alliances.

- Bill from WMI exemplifies the power of leveraging relationships for growth, mirroring Atlassian's partner-first approach, which has been fundamental to their market success.

- The "Five 'P's of Partnering" present a clear framework for building effective alliances, emphasizing the importance of aligning values, team strengths, partnership appreciation, process efficiency, and shared planning for a prosperous collaboration.

Partnership Road Map—Action Steps

1. *Assess your partnering maturity and focus needs based on the 5Ps checklist in this chapter.* Identify the areas you most need to improve AND the areas you are already doing well with so that you can keep leveraging those areas.

2. *Develop a partner-centric culture and people strategy.* Cultivate a company culture that is conducive to partnering by training and selecting individuals who exhibit the necessary personalities, competencies, and skills for partner-facing roles. Define clear leadership for partnership initiatives and establish visible accountability structures. This step also involves creating a hiring profile that targets individuals who can thrive in a partner-centric environment. Cultivate a high-trust, collaborative internal culture that encourages engagement and teamwork. Actively work to integrate this culture into all levels of the organization and ensure that it is reflected in the approach to partnerships.

3. *Align your organization's leadership and team members to adopt a partner-centric mindset, prioritizing the development of strategic partnerships that align with long-term business goals and shared visions for market expansion.*

4. Build your measure of Partner LifeTime Value® effectively and use this metric to guide strategic decisions. Focus on long-term partnership value and invest in building relationships that are likely to contribute to sustained growth and profitability.

119

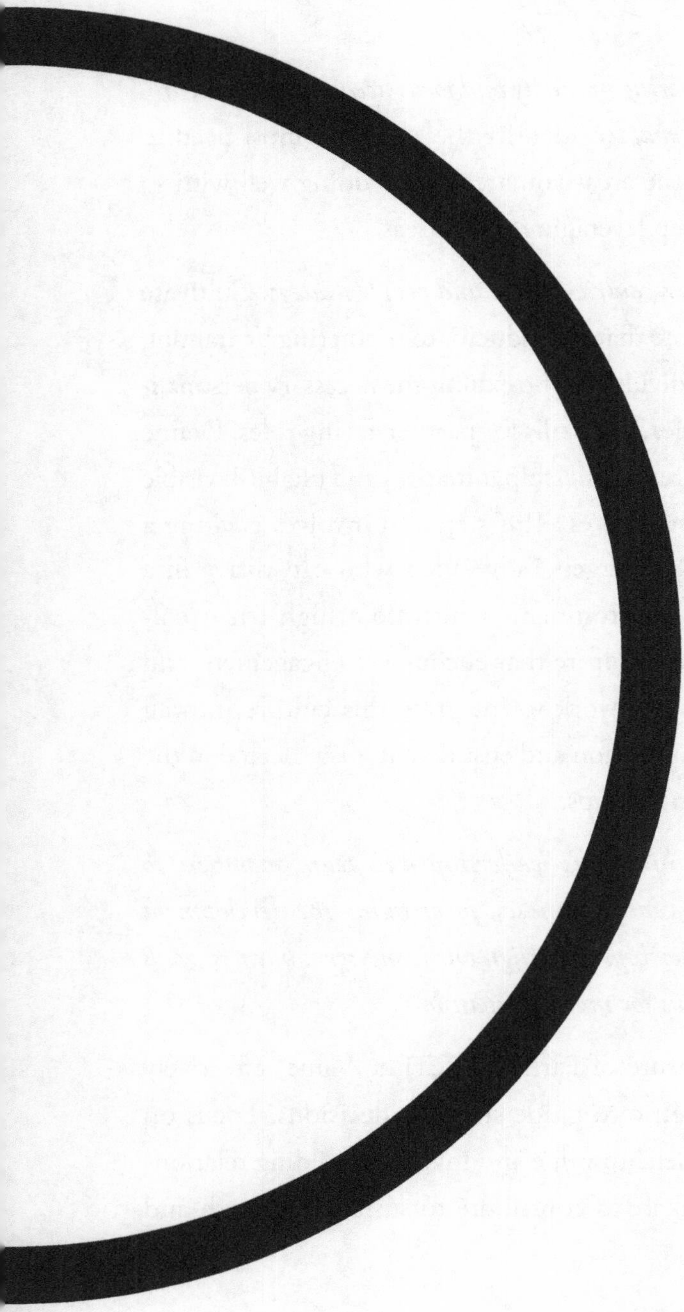

CHAPTER 9

THE PRINCIPLES, PROCESSES, AND PLANNING FOR PARTNER LIFETIME VALUE® PARTNERING

"The best partnerships are those where both parties benefit and where the whole is greater than the sum of its parts."

–MICHAEL EISNER, FORMER CEO OF DISNEY

In this chapter, we explore the complexities of joint business planning and the transformative shift from simple transactions to strategic partnerships, drawing from Michael Eisner's insights on the collective power of collaboration. Emphasizing a partner-centric approach, we discuss how to cultivate enduring partnerships that contribute to long-term success and market expansion. We delve into selecting and nurturing "partners for life" who share aligned goals and visions and empower pivotal team members to navigate and shape these alliances. The chapter also contrasts different business models, underscoring the need for compatibility to drive mutual growth and accelerate business objectives.

Partnering is much more than sales improvements. Ideally, the CEO or president asks the entire leadership team to be truly devoted to a partner-focused approach across the company with employees, with clients and customers, suppliers, and partners. A true and sincere partner-focused approach goes beyond basic terms like distribution network, franchise, agent, doctor, channel, dealer in name only. This enlightened way of life sees partnerships as more than just delegated tasks; they are passionate alliances built on trust, common objectives, and shared rewards. True partnering means nurturing real connections, candid talks, and teamwork toward shared goals and vision.

A partner-centric growth strategy acknowledges that organizations thrive through collaboration, not in isolation. Despite emphasizing values like customer service and quality, the importance of partnering is often overlooked. Partnering aligns interests, leverages strengths, and tackles challenges together, unlocking synergies and broader market reach. This strategy builds lasting relationships and a thriving ecosystem for mutual success, harnessing combined resources and networks to create exceptional value.

Principles: Just as every organization needs partnering, every organization needs Partnering Principles.

Pat Doherty, CRO of Flexential, explains: If partnering feels like "Just Another Selling Mechanism, then they will use you opportunistically. Developing productive relationships needs to be done proactively. This sets the stage to manage through conflicts."

You see companies achieving higher rates of revenue growth and profitability when the organizations get partnering correct and *publicly acknowledge their commitment to a mindset of partnering success across their customers, employees, partners, and suppliers.*

Dave Raftery is a former chief revenue officer at Integration Partners who helped build the company and take it to an exit. One of his core philosophies, since the time he joined when the organization was $5M, was that relationships matter, people matter, and partnerships matter. He first built the Midwest office into a successful division then expanded his role as sales leader with a core philosophy that if you partner with your clients instead of selling to your clients, you will win over your competition. Integration Partners was acquired by ConvergeOne. This example reinforces the strategic imperative— every company no matter big or small needs to partner; and if you partner you must get partnering right.

Ron Rohner, often regarded as a visionary pioneer of technology channels, embarked on his illustrious career at Apple as employee 86 and Executive Number 8, where he honed his expertise in channels while they were still developing as a field. Over the span of thirty-five-plus years, he cultivated his consultancy, becoming a guiding force for major technology leaders and their intricate partnering endeavor. Ron advocates that certain considerations are critical for any executive considering this strategy. As you can see Ron's key considerations below align with many of the key ideas reinforced in this book. How many of these have you adopted as a guiding principle in your organization? This is an *acknowledgment that partners are* critical to long-term success for all or part of your organization's operations.

- *Smart partnering defines success:* Recognition that effective partnering strategy will result in better outcomes to more end customers, and more loyal customers long term.

- *Partners are an asset:* Your partners are an asset and a profit contributor, not a liability or an expense when you do this right.

- *Think long term:* Acceptance that partnering may require foregoing some short-term gains in exchange for long-term value.

- *Patience pays off:* You recognize that investments in partnering take time to show positive results, even months or years.

- *Partnering is not a straight line:* Acceptance that partnering is not a linear relationship and often involves a complex ecosystem of participants and organizations that must be embraced for success.

- *Partnering with customers, partners, suppliers, and one another is key:* You acknowledge that your partners (treating customers like partners, your partners treating you as a true partner) are all critical to short- and long-term success.

- *Partnering is a company-wide effort:* It covers everything from making products, packaging solutions, planning how to sell them, and helping customers achieve their goals. It is collaborative, and spans from product development to market planning, to product packaging, and to customer support.

You can also see that each of these requires the process and structure behind it to make these principles a reality. That's why processes and programs go hand in hand with guiding principles. Both processes and programs allow you as a company to build trust at scale and allow you to build repeatable business models and recurring revenue. I was on a Disney Cruise, and I was astounded at the number of partner relationships that Disney had with beverage companies, toy companies, jewelry companies, and credit card and flight companies. And they made partnering and spending money with these companies easy and flawless for the cruise consumer.

Stable and open PROCESSES should foster partner managers to become trusted advisors and true value-added support.

Processes should be additive to the relationships and streamline activities and make business easier. Good Partnering Processes should build not erode trust! In today's digital age, artificial intelligence, automation tools, and advanced partner relationship management systems offer a powerful combination to personalize partner experiences while maintaining efficiency at scale. For the greatest impact, these systems should be cocreated with partners, incorporating their insights to ensure alignment with their needs.

Consider the scenario where a supplier rolls out a new order system without consulting integrators, only to discover they juggle multiple systems from other suppliers. Such a system is unlikely to be welcomed.

Distributors and wholesalers, as vital intermediaries, have traditionally added value by streamlining processes such as inventory management, order placement, and billing. Similarly, aggregators play a crucial role in simplifying procurement and the supply chain.

A mentor once advised me to ask partners to identify their top suppliers, integrators, or customers and to dig into the reasons behind their choices. Understanding what sets these entities apart can be transformative and should inform strategic priorities alongside in-depth assessments.

Case Study in Action:

Here's a successful partnering example at a large corporation: At Verizon, John Constantino realized that Verizon Business had an opportunity to reach even more small and midsize business customers via a partner-based mindset. Verizon was well positioned with large enterprise coverage and with con-

sumer-oriented service and sales centers, but there was a growth opportunity in the small and midsize business market. After careful analysis, he saw that partnering with direct and indirect sellers would be vital to Verizon Business's success in the market.

Since launching this partner-focused approach to the small and midsize business market three years ago, John has seen dramatic results. His focus on partners and integrating Verizon Business and processes into their business and growth initiatives resulted in business growth across his teams and initiatives at a rate 2–3× faster than Verizon's general growth. According to John, his work with partners will enable even more growth opportunities as small and midsize businesses adopt solutions that Verizon Business previously offered only to enterprises. Another proof point that even the largest companies who get partnering right will prosper well above and beyond the norm.

Working with partners seamlessly requires a culture of collaboration. When you create a high-trust, high-Partnering Growth DNA inside the organization as discussed earlier, you have more engaged employees and higher-functioning teams.

Imagine an organization attempting to grow that gets the executive team aligned around partnerships and built into the organizational DNA. The organization's CEO, CRO, CMO, CFO, SVP of Engineering, and the chief legal counsel are each committed to making strategic partners successful. The enthusiasm of the C-suite will spread lightning-fast inside of your organization and across your partners as well.

Partner LifeTime Value® is about prioritizing partner retention and mutual success. It's determined by two things: how much partners produce each year and how long they stay partners. In simpler terms, it's the total revenue and profit generated by a partner throughout their partnership.

Partner LifeTime Value®

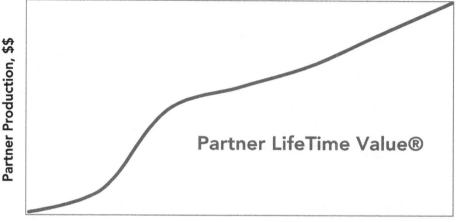

Partner Lifespan, Years

The partner-centric DNA is fast becoming a differentiator for organizations. According to Anatomy of Work, cultures of high collaboration create higher-growth organizations. High-collaboration cultures were 79 percent more likely to feel prepared to respond to business challenges than laggard organizations. And 92 percent of organizations with high cross-functional collaboration felt they were contributing valuable work (compared to 50 percent for laggards). Furthermore, 55 percent of the high-collaboration cultures had revenue growth year over year versus only 20 percent of the low-collaboration organizations.

The entire organization must embrace and advance partnering. A partnering culture is the means to business growth.

-Ron Rohner,
CEO, Rohner & Associates

An AchieveUnite study with the University of Glasgow shows that when Partner LifeTime Value® is the motivation for a partner-centric strategy, the case for cultural alignment is a no-brainer. The questions to be asked and answered are:

- How can we help our partners be more productive?

- How do we help them optimize *their* Customer LifeTime Value?

- How can we select, retain, and develop the highest-growth, most productive partners?

- How can we ensure that when our partners grow, we grow? When we grow, our partners grow?

Christian Alvarez, CRO at Stratasys, a true partner of AchieveUnite, and a partnering industry expert has five *Partnering Truths*:

1. *NO matter what industry you are in, it's all about solutions. It's no longer about the product you are selling.* Verticals matter like aerospace, manufacturing, and healthcare. How you adopt a solution is critical. This is one reason why partnering is critical. And the old ways of supplier-to-supplier transactions are outdated.

2. *It's also about business solutions:* Processes like deal registration, supplier RFPs are fast becoming outdated. It's about innovating and prototyping and building partner relationships that foster that level of innovation. Your customer and partner experience can be a differentiator and a key part of the solution—not just the solution itself.

3. *When you partner, you need to be an extension of one another's whole organization.* But it's more than that—it's our values, our vision, our joint goals. We need to be an extension of each other's culture.

4. *Companies must take a lifetime value approach.* You must do your best to get out of the quarterly view only for these relationships. It needs to be longer—one word: lifetime. It's critical to look at what's happening in today's consumption- and subscription-based economy. How customers are selecting, procuring, and consuming business services has evolved. And now it's subscription, and it's consumption. It's about the lifetime value of that customer. In many industries, you see five-, eight-, nine-year life cycles. You're talking about renewals, expand modernization, and do that all over again.

5. *It's about the infinity-loop life cycle of the customer and there could be three to five partner companies involved in the solution or more.* The infinity loop represents the power of combining

129

organizations' joint value and producing a unified strategy and program where the whole is greater than the sum of the parts.

This infinity loop can be used as a brainstorming exercise with your most valuable partners to consistently expand revenue, iterate, and improve joint solutions and new market opportunities.

The Infinite Loop of Collaboration

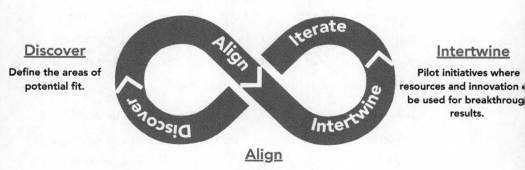

Discover
Define the areas of potential fit.

Align

Iterate

Intertwine
Pilot initiatives where resources and innovation be used for breakthrough results.

Align
Document the priority areas for joint investments with the partner.

Once the initial interdependence experiment is complete and measured, it is time to re-engage at the discovery phase again, and so on.

Key Takeaways from Chapter 9

- Emphasizing the Partner LifeTime Value® concept, the chapter highlights the importance of focusing on the long-term value and mutual success that partners bring to the organization. This approach goes beyond mere revenue generation and looks at the overall contribution and growth potential of the partnership over its entire life span. By amplifying this message both internally and externally, companies can reinforce the significance of partnerships and ensure that both the organization and its partners understand and commit to this long-term, value-based strategy.

- *Long-Term Value Focus:* Prioritize the long-term success and growth potential inherent in partnerships, recognizing that cultivating enduring relationships contributes more significantly to the organization's progress than short-term gains.

- *Collaborative Culture Is Crucial:* A collaborative culture that emphasizes cross-functional teamwork and values partner contributions is essential for responding to business challenges and achieving sustainable revenue growth.

Partnering Road Map—Action Steps

1. *Cultivate Partnership Commitment.* Instill a partnership-first mindset at all company levels, ensuring leadership actively promotes and participates in fostering meaningful relationships with all partners.

2. *Refine Partner Processes.* Regularly review and cocreate processes with partners to streamline efficiency and alignment, utilizing advanced tools to personalize the partner experience.

3. *Evaluate and Grow Partner Value.* Adopt metrics for assessing Partner LifeTime Value® and prioritize initiatives that enhance long-term partnership success and revenue opportunities.

CHAPTER 10
ESSENTIALS OF BUILDING PARTNERSHIPS

ALIGNING PEOPLE AND PARTNERS

By embracing a partner-centric approach, organizations can transcend traditional sales tactics to forge alliances rooted in shared success and longevity. You have navigated through the principles and practices that elevate partnerships to strategic assets, highlighting the significance of aligning with partners' visions and goals. As you move beyond the pages of this chapter, the key takeaway is clear: invest in the relationship equity of partnerships, and understand the depths of how to build partnerships for innovation, growth, and sustained mutual value. The journey of partnership is ongoing, a continuous cycle of alignment, execution, and celebration—a pathway to collective achievement and prosperity.

Partnerships can be likened to an orchestra performance where two or more musicians make music in a synchronized and harmonious manner. In an orchestra, you see strings, brass, and percussion combining to produce a result that neither, acting alone, could do.

In the context of partnerships, this analogy represents the ongoing cycle of collaboration, communication, and mutual support. Just as musicians must stay in sync with each other, partners in a successful collaboration must maintain constant interaction and alignment.

When done right, successful partnerships create a sense of fulfillment, achievement, and shared success. The interplay of trust, cooperation, and shared vision allows partners to create something greater together.

High front-line empowerment in companies correlates with increased partnering success, resulting in overall revenue and profit growth. To achieve exponential partnering-driven growth, it's crucial to empower and educate sales, marketing, corporate executives, and support teams, ensuring their active involvement in the organizational learning process. The sellers must have an advanced level of partnering expertise—more than ever before. It's about the customer journey and the adoption and leverage of partners throughout that journey. The Partnering Success methodology has fast become another foundational element for every seller.

Let's look at Carahsoft Technology Corp., Trusted Public Sector IT Solutions Provider®, supporting the United States of America's federal and state government departments, local county and city agencies, education, and healthcare markets. Founded in 2004 by Craig Abod, Carahsoft currently employs more than two thousand professionals dedicated to serving customers and partners. Craig teaches every employee that Carahsoft exists to serve three partner constituents: government entities; technology supplier corporations and service providers; and the partner integrators of technology serving governments, education, and healthcare. This task is considerable when you realize the number of different business models and priorities.

He strives to build partnering muscles into the DNA of every employee, their interactions, and Carahsoft's service offerings. Craig walks the talk. He has built an energetic team well-known among the

US government community. Carahsoft's successful growth as a private company is proof of his three-pronged partnering approach.

Like Craig does so well, organizations that desire partnering success need to select and train partner managers, sellers, and marketing teams. All people associated with partnering, even procurement specialists, need to be trained in partnering methods. It's a fundamental shift from the RFP, the quotation, and the old way of doing business.

Case Study in Action:

Nate Olsen, currently EVP, JESAM Enterprises LLC, a growth advisory services consulting firm, has over twenty-five years' experience in sales of HR Outsourced Services. During the latter phase of his sales career, Nate spearheaded partner development at a $6 billion, publicly traded professional employer organization (PEO), a leader in delivering HR Outsourced Services to small and medium-sized enterprises. Nate coined the term "co-selling," though he later came to recognize that genuine partnering went beyond the confines of co-selling. According to Nate, "Partnering is about sharing resources for common purposes. At our company, we realized that our traditional direct sales representatives needed to be transformed to become partnering success managers." To signify the mindset change, and at Nate's direction, the role of AchieveUnite Partner Performance Advisor was created. At the time of the book's publication, this designation has been given to over two thousand individuals who have grown their skills in partnering to become true strategic advisors.

Next, Nate realized that a comprehensive training initiative would help shift the organization's traditional sales behavior. The training began with self-assessment evaluation involving eighty potential partner managers. The self-assessment focused on three core dimensions of the partner manager's skill set: knowledge of partnering principles, willingness to collaborate, and business success understanding. As a general trend, participants initially ranked themselves highest in collaboration skills and lowest in business success understanding. After the workshops, participants retook the self-assessment evaluation to see how they had improved their skills in the three partnering competencies: a sample before and after self-assessment is shown below.

Partnering Competency Awareness Assessment

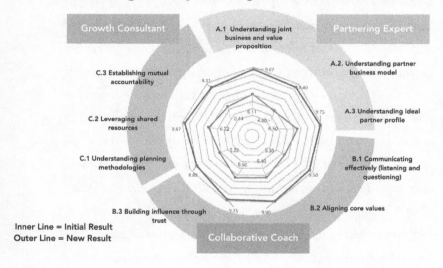

Inner Line = Initial Result
Outer Line = New Result

Of the nine factors included in the self-assessment, the two lowest were:

- Understanding Partner Business Model at 4.80 of 10

- Understanding Planning Methodologies at 5.22 of 10

These factors are most related to the B2B connection with the partner, Business Accelerator. The highest ratings were in collaboration, which is a relationship factor. It makes sense that potential partner managers would consider themselves good at building relationships. The surprise was the low scoring when evaluating themselves in understanding and influencing the partner's business. Once they realized the actions they should be taking, the scores increased. After participating in AchieveUnite education, assessment scores of the three primary skills increased on average 32 percent.

In addition to the Partner Performance Advisor certification program from AchieveUnite, Nate worked with AchieveUnite to segment partners based on their profiles and success criteria. He knew that differing partner businesses were interested in differing relationships, designed to deliver differing results. Over the five-year span of his leadership, partner-sourced annual sales grew from zero to over 60 percent of the organization's annual sales.

Tim McCarthy, vice president at Biscayne Contractors, Inc. said that working with his government clients and suppliers is all about partnering. He selects and focuses on how his partners tick and what matters to them. He knows their goals as a company, and he knows his partner executive's personal goals as well. He and his company pride themselves on building a partnership with every federal government client they work with. One of his clients said, "Tim, you are one of the only companies who truly partners with us and understands what matters to us and why. It's much more than a contract for you."

All three of these examples illustrate the criticality of "partnering success skills" becoming embedded and truly a strong muscle for every team member. Now this varies by role—some skills like trust-building, influence, joint value propositions and business propositions transcend every role in the company. Other skills are specific to the roles like the example you see here for co-selling and partnering success managers.

Navigating Losses and Partnering Challenges with Exceptional Responses

When confronted with losses or breaches in partnering agreements, an exceptional response is not just warranted—it's essential. Imagine a scenario at a high-end restaurant where the service and meal preparation fall short of expectations. A competent server may acknowledge the issue and attempt a resolution. However, an exemplary manager will go beyond mere acknowledgment—they will deliver a response so unexpectedly generous that the customer feels compelled to share the experience with others.

As you assume the role of a trusted business advisor, understand that the path is fraught with challenges. Relationships ebb and flow, as do the fortunes of any team—celebrating wins and enduring losses. The occurrence of a loss should not catch you off guard. Instead, it is a critical moment to demonstrate your ability to leverage successes and, more importantly, to confront losses head-on. This involves drawing upon the difficult conversation techniques emphasized earlier in this book.

I have personally encountered missed opportunities due to unrecognized frustration or inadequately handled challenging discussions. It is these moments that underscore the importance of embracing difficult conversations and accepting negative feedback or bad news with openness and transparency. As once imparted by a distinguished professor at Georgetown University, feedback should be seen as a gift; its utilization is at your discretion. When adverse situations arise, it's crucial to operate transparently, act quickly and judiciously, and err on the side of honest communications with all parties.

Many have learned through hard experience that mishandling situations in real time can lead to lasting damage or, worse, a broken partnership. George Hope, former EMC, HPE Executive, and Infoblox Revenue Leader, wisely observes that the true measure of a partnership is its resilience in weathering bad news and still maintaining the commitment to work together. He often says that we have to drive and live on the two-way street and give the same as what we expect from our partners.

After establishing personal relationships and trust with your partner, the subsequent objective is to gain a profound understanding of your partner's business model, operational mechanisms, and the challenges they face. It is through this deep understanding that you can truly align your responses with the needs and expectations of the partnership, thus strengthening the collaborative bond even in the face of adversity. This is a level deeper than the surface transparency as well—and it is here immense joint value often lies.

Here are lessons learned:

- Find opportunities to celebrate small wins early on in a partnership.

- Create small, short-term, joint goals.

- Celebrate the success together with larger cross-functional teams.

PARTNERS are the lifeblood of growth for any organization looking to build new markets.

This P particularly refers to external partnerships and/or building your customer relationships into partnerships. Partnerships are also critical to maintain in an M&A integration—and this is a place where many companies go wrong and lose momentum with partners if not handled correctly.

Case Study in Action:

Nick Tidd, former vice president, Global Channel Sales at Poly, has been involved in eight business integrations—the most recent is when he led the integration of Poly and HP. He shares his seven thoughts on how to ensure your and your partner's initiatives are successful in the integration.

1. Partners need confidence knowing their investments will be protected. These investments have different meanings for different organizations—some come from a value model and others from a volume model. It is important to understand partners' pain points—knowing you can't solve for all of them—and address the pain that you can.

2. Leverage for scale. Just because you may be the smaller of the two organizations in an integration, there are a lot of best practices that you can offer because you are smaller and possibly nimbler. Don't be afraid to share best practice, but don't get stuck in "the way we've always done it." Look at it through a different lens. Think about the different routes to market.

3. Adopt and micromanage the change management programs. Communicate, but give yourself space knowing there will be directional changes along the way. For example, most partner programs pay rebates. How one vendor values a dollar may be different from how the other vendor values the dollar. Be careful about publishing rate tables, percentages of revenue, and MDF. Communicate the concept and fill in the detail later.

4. Test your assumptions and test them often—internally and externally. Communicate the changes and know that things will take longer to complete than you expect.

5. Move fast, but not too fast. In medium and large partnering integrations, if you try to integrate all regions and all countries at the same time, you will fail.

6. Communicate. Cascade your decisions in a precise manner and often so that everybody stays aligned. Alignment is key to an acquisition. And where possible put people full time on integrations.

7. Finally, hold on to your key talent. Listen to them and communicate with them.

Earning Your Seat at the Table as a Trusted Business Advisor

A trusted business advisor surpasses being a mere supplier or problem solver, maintaining their role by consistently adding value and contributing to success. They are expected to understand your products, business objectives, and excel in various aspects, such as business operations, financial statements, and HR management. Their expertise extends to incorporating innovative ideas from business media and research, crucial for attaining the trusted business advisor position, which hinges on aligning your business with your partner's. If you aspire to be a trusted business advisor but haven't accomplished that with your partner yet, consider who else fills the role for that person.

Perhaps you can ask the partner business owner or executive, "Who do you go to for business advice?" It might be a relative, or a banker, or a lawyer, or a friend in a similar business.

Follow with, "What do you and your advisor talk about?" Answers to these two questions will light the path to your seat at his/her table as well.

The Target is the True Seat at the Table

You're talking about the table at which the partner's strategic decisions are made. You say "earn" because these seats are not given away or won in a lottery; they are granted to those who have value and are viewed as equal participants. As a trusted business advisor, a seat at the table is a reasonable expectation. Earlier we discussed the education programs to help you earn the seat at the table, and this is about recognizing whether you have the seat at the table and how to strengthen that.

Checklist of a Partner with a Seat at the Table

What do partners want from a supplier who is sitting at their table?

☐ I am someone who can make or influence supplier (partner) decisions.

☐ I am someone who can marshal supplier resources when needed for the good of the partnership.

☐ I am someone who understands the supplier's products and services, in concert with the business strategy of the partner.

☐ I am someone who has good business acumen and can bring innovative suggestions to the table.

☐ I am someone who the executive team will include in critical customer and partner events.

☐ And above all I am someone who can be trusted beyond any doubt.

Selecting the Right Partners is essential; all partners are not created equal and of equal opportunity and importance.

Crafting a robust customer sales pipeline is analogous to developing a partner sales pipeline, yet the latter demands a more strategic and long-term outlook. The essence of a successful partner pipeline lies in cultivating relationships that transcend transactional interactions and evolve into enduring partnerships.

To achieve this, it is essential to carefully curate a selection of potential partners who exemplify the ideal of partners for life, or partner lifetime value. These are entities aligned not only with your immediate goals but also with your vision for future growth. Be it suppliers contributing to a novel product line or integrators broadening your reach into new markets, the synergy must be rooted in a shared commitment to a mutually beneficial and explicitly articulated objective.

The recruitment, selection, and onboarding of partners, coupled with fostering their initial success, are processes that require meticulous planning and execution. This strategic endeavor should never be left to chance; it demands thoughtful consideration and execution at every juncture to ensure alignment with your overarching business goals.

It is very important to identify your best fit partners. No one can be everything to every partner or every person in the partner; so, it's critical for you to pick wisely these partners, and the people in the partner. Below are some techniques to help you align with your ideal partner.

It is not just about devising the right strategy but also about impeccable execution. A well-defined and carefully implemented partner strategy is the linchpin of a thriving, sustainable partnership ecosystem.

Pathway to Partnering Success

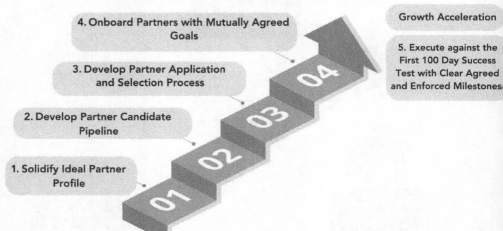

4. Onboard Partners with Mutually Agreed Goals

3. Develop Partner Application and Selection Process

2. Develop Partner Candidate Pipeline

1. Solidify Ideal Partner Profile

Growth Acceleration

5. Execute against the First 100 Day Success Test with Clear Agreed and Enforced Milestones

The discovery phase involves the people responsible for owning the partnership development area—this could be the seller, the partner manager, the procurement leader, the owner of the company. You refer to them as the "front-liners"—they are the owners of the relationship and accountable for the success. Front-liners must be empowered to make partnership decisions and facilitate the progression and growth with the partner. It's important that there are clear partner investment decisions that can be made by the front-liners and only the most significant decisions get escalated to the "boss."

Kristi Kirby, senior executive in sales and marketing at one of the largest global distributors in the world, believes that if she empowers her team to really uncover the benefit to both the partner and the vendor, her company wins too. She encourages her team to take risks, to plan with partners, and to be creative to solve challenges. Kristi has also been extremely diligent and successful at packaging each step in the above process with clear steps, milestones, and rewards. She empowers her team at each level and is there for the large escalations. In newly minted partnerships, trust is often untested. The leaders of each partner organization may have different motivations, the companies—different business models.

Partnering Different Business Models

So, if you are horizontal and your partner is vertical, how do you best intersect these two different business types to work together? The answer is that mutually successful partnerships require an unprecedented level of transparency to see the areas of commonality, and they require organizational trust. *Open dialogue and organizational trust are critical for both the strategic definition and execution of the partnership.*

Extreme partnership and organizational trust—that is what is required by all parties to coordinate all these layers, so they appear seamless to the outside, and so that all parties realize the intended results. Businesses in the horizontal space focused on scale, volume, cost, and quality need to understand the priorities of the vertical entities, which are focused on customer-specific, tailored, value-add solutions, and vice versa.

Partners should be chosen strategically, like how Venture Capitalists or Private Equity firms carefully select companies for their portfolios. Both small and large organizations need to establish a formal process for partner recruitment. It's crucial to recognize that not all partners are willing to build a close, trusting relationship, be open to growth opportunities, or share their financials for collaborative investment. To adopt a portfolio approach, partnering organizations must thoroughly understand the partner's business model and analyze alignment and intersection phases.

Fit Is Critical and Often Underestimated

Since partners have unique criteria and preferences, it's wise to customize how to assess and reward them based on their specific needs. Suppliers, integrators, and customers all see their businesses as unique, yet are often treated the same way.

In order to cultivate a successful partnership, it is imperative to deeply understand how your business model intersects with those of your partners. This graphic illustrates the areas of overlap between the Supplier, Integrator, and Customer business models. It serves as a guide for identifying the shared spaces where collaborative efforts and strategic alignments can be optimized for mutual benefit, thereby enhancing the synergy and effectiveness of the partnership.

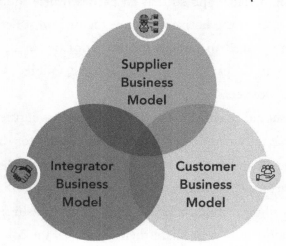

For example, some businesses are oriented to standardized products, volume operations, and scale economics. They operate *horizontally*. Most manufacturers, product companies, and large service companies operate in a scale model that requires heavy investment up front. To maximize profit, scale businesses focus on volume of units sold to achieve revenue goals.

Semiconductor is one example. Intel and TSMC build a new manufacturing facility for $10B or more. The first chip requires a big investment. Not so the second, and third, and fourth, etc. Other examples of scale business models are all around: Ford, GM, Toyota, and KIA in automotive; General Mills, InBev, Coca Cola, and P&G in consumer products; and Cessna, Piper, and Beechcraft in private aircraft.

Other firms create value by customizing their products or services to meet the specific needs of individual clients. These companies focus on a particular industry or client segment. Professional services firms, such as systems integrators, financial advisors, and consulting firms, are examples of *vertically* oriented businesses. These businesses specialize in understanding the unique circumstances and requirements of clients. They develop and provide tailored solutions. Vertical businesses must deliver targeted solutions that yield measurable results for their clients to build profitability.

Some firms operate with a combination of horizontal and vertical components. The dilemma is that at two ends of the spectrum, you get two different business models with totally different motivations: volume versus value. Suppliers are typically volume participants. Integrators rely on value, or a vertical approach. Of course, you know that many companies fall in the middle of these two extremes. You even see *hybrids*, called "*Vertizontals*," a combination of vertical and horizontal business models.

Vertizontal-Meshing Two Economic Models

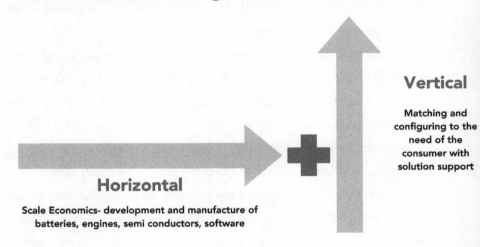

Vertical

Matching and
configuring to the
need of the
consumer with
solution support

Horizontal

Scale Economics- development and manufacture of
batteries, engines, semi conductors, software

In these "vertizontal" examples, some firms decide to operate sister divisions or groups, one focusing on the horizontal and the other on the vertical.

The moral of this story is to explore the business model of your partners to discover the intersection or overlap. It is at that very intersection where real business value and acceleration exists.

Partnerships are most beneficial when they help both organizations and all the organizations involved in the network achieve "leverage." Leverage in this case means that the growth sustained by the partnership has a ripple effect, a wide and expanded impact.

Partnerships exist in many forms. Loretta McCarthy is the co-CEO and managing partner of Golden Seeds. She leads an early-stage investment firm focused on providing capital and support to women entrepreneurs as they launch and grow their businesses. When asked about working with partners, Loretta said,

"Influencing and leading partners is very different from directing employees. In any organization, employees have much

in common with their leaders: value statements, compensation plans, periodic goals, established culture, and acceptable behaviors.

"When working with partners, too often we assume that the partner is motivated by the same success criteria as we are. Totally wrong. This assumption sets the partnership up for failure, or at a minimum, sub-optimization. Instead, before we engage with partners, be they suppliers, customers, or contracted support, find out what makes them tick, personally and business wise. If not a fit, find a better fit."

Loretta often works with her early-stage portfolio companies to find fractional executive support resources. She commented that when you need a CFO, for example, but can't afford one, hire one-third of the CFO. To Loretta, fractional executive support is a form of partner engagement. Personality, commitment, and competency are the three keys to finding the chemistry that works in Loretta's experience.

After listening to partners, I modified the business unit's operational metrics and go-to-market approach to better align with the way our partners want to do business.

-John Muscarella,
VP, Channel Sales at Cox Business

As this chapter closes, let's reiterate the profound significance of cultivating strategic partnerships, which are not merely conduits for immediate gain but pivotal for long-term growth and innovation. The journey of nurturing these relationships requires a meticulous blend of strategy and execution, with an unwavering commitment to mutual success. By fostering an ecosystem where trust, transparency, and shared goals are the foundation, organizations can achieve unprecedented levels of constructive collaboration and acceleration. Whether through the fusion of "vertizontal" business models or the tailored approach of front-liners empowering partnerships, the goal remains steadfast: to forge alliances that propel both entities toward a future where their combined strengths create a sum greater than their parts. In this symbiotic evolution, each partner thrives, leveraged by the other's success, fostering a network of relationships that become instrumental in sculpting the landscape of industry and innovation. This is the essence of a partnership mindset, where the pursuit of common ambitions ensures that every handshake is a promise of progress, and every collaboration is a step toward a shared horizon.

Key Takeaways from Chapter 10

- The success of a partnership heavily relies on the empowerment of the front-liners. These individuals are accountable for the relationship's success and must be trusted to make significant partnership decisions. Their autonomy allows for swift and effective action, reserving only the most critical decisions for higher management.

- A thorough understanding of both partners' business models is imperative for successful partnerships, especially when different models (horizontal versus vertical) intersect. Identifying common goals and areas of overlap is crucial, and this requires a high degree of transparency and organizational trust.

- *Partnerships* benefit greatly when they are customized to meet the specific criteria and preferences of each party involved. This bespoke approach, advocated by leaders like Kristi Kirby and Loretta McCarthy, acknowledges the unique nature of each business and allows for partnerships that genuinely add value, promoting growth and leverage within the ecosystem.

Ask Yourself

Partner's Business	Answer
What are the preferred end markets?	
What are the Strategic Competencies?	
What are the partner support needs?	
How can the partnership be configured for competitive advantange?	

What is the partner's appetite for a close relationship?	
How open is the partner to joint activities with customers?	
How do the partner's products and services complement the supplier's current and future planned capabilities?	

https://www.achieveunite.com/partneringsuccessbookresources/

Partnership Road Map—Action Steps

1. *Refine Partner Profiling and Recruitment.* Establish a robust process for identifying and engaging potential partners who are aligned with the organization's strategic objectives and have the potential to be "partners for life." This involves creating a detailed partner profile that includes not just business goals but also cultural fit and long-term value alignment. Use this profile to recruit, select, and onboard partners deliberately, ensuring they integrate well into the existing ecosystem and are set up for early successes.

2. *Empower and Support Front-Line Staff.* Define clear roles, responsibilities, and decision-making powers for those directly involved in partnership development, such as partner managers and sales teams. Provide them with the

tools, authority, and support they need to foster and manage these relationships effectively. Ensure they have the capacity to make on-the-spot decisions that are conducive to the partnership's growth, requiring only the most significant decisions to be escalated.

3. *Facilitate Transparent and Strategic Partner Engagements:* Develop a system of open communication and trust with partners, recognizing the diverse business models and motivations that each partner brings to the table. Create forums for strategic dialogue and collaboration that allow partners to understand mutual business models, identify common goals, and explore areas for joint value creation. This approach will help both horizontal and vertical businesses to work together more effectively, aligning volume and value motivations for mutual benefit.

PART 4

COMMUNITY INFLUENCE

CHAPTER 11

COMMUNITY ORCHESTRATION

THE KEYSTONE OF ECOSYSTEM INNOVATION AND POWER

Community Orchestration is a critical element for business growth, detailed as the third dimension in this book. It's about how organizations network, learn from each other, and collectively accelerate growth. Here, you'll see how partnerships are more than just connections—they're a support system that thrives on shared interests and goals. This section breaks down how these relationships work and how they can adapt to external pressures like market shifts and regulatory changes. Get ready for practical insights on building, participating, and thriving with business communities—a subset of the ecosystem.

Ecosystems are like the universe. Communities are subsets of the universe, a subset that is closest to you, your business, your partners. It is these communities that are important to understand, define, and influence. Ecosystems are made up of communities. Ecosystems thrive on the intricate relationships between different organizations, and they rely on a complex network of interconnected relationships and interactions to sustain forward movement. The organizations comprising an ecosystem community rely on each other for resources, support, and growth.

Ecosystems are also affected by external factors such as new business models, regulations, and economics, which, in turn, affect all organizations that are part of the community. While these influences can't be controlled, they can be acknowledged and influenced. In chapters 8–10, we explored the sources of influence and techniques that can be used to affect partner behavior and reinforce partner commitment.

Think of this as the ecosystem of organizations who provide the following:

- Common interests and thought leadership for partners

- Collaborative learning opportunities for partners

- Growth acceleration for all partners

- Networking opportunities with partners

- Ideas and mechanisms for expansion of partners' businesses

- Recognition, rewards, and prestige for partners in the ecosystem

Your partner community is a subset of the larger ecosystem. It is a network of businesses, organizations, and individuals that provide delivery of a specific product or service through advice, influence, and cooperation. Each aspect of the community impacts and is impacted by the others. In short if you want to differentiate yourself, scale faster, and beat out your competitors, partner communities are a MUST HAVE. Note: Partner communities are more than just the group of your partners. In the rapidly evolving landscape of modern business, understanding and leveraging the influence of communities is crucial for success. This chapter delves into the vital role that these groups play as drivers of customer preferences, market trends, and strategic partnerships. You will uncover how businesses can tap into the power of these networks to forge stronger connections, make informed decisions, and stay ahead in a competitive market.

Communities of Influence

In earlier chapters, Relationship Development and Business Acceleration were discussed. You gained assessments, tools, and techniques to help enhance Partner LifeTime Value®. You also were introduced to the idea of different forms and types of strategic partnerships for different purposes and the importance of the ecosystem.

In communities, you will see an ever-evolving world of influences affecting customer needs, digital complements, new competition, and a variety of other easily accessible messaging. While you may have heard this broader environment referred to as "ecosystems," here they are referred to as *communities of influence*.

"You should try not to control communities, only understand their influences, and add your voice to the narrative," said Rod Baptie, founder and owner of Baptie & Co. Rod has spent more than thirty years being the catalyst for innovative discussion of like-positioned technology organizations.

The wisdom Rod Baptie shares comes from a wealth of experience in fostering communities where control is less about wielding power and more about understanding the ebb and flow of collective dynamics. His company, Baptie & Co., thrives by recognizing that communities—especially those in fast-evolving sectors like technology and telecommunications—are organic entities with their own cultures, behaviors, and influence patterns. Understanding these elements is crucial for anyone looking to engage with such communities meaningfully. By grasping the underlying currents that drive a community, one can effectively contribute to the ongoing narrative, shaping discussions and outcomes not through force, but through informed participation and contribution. This approach champions a symbiotic relationship where the community's growth and the individual's objectives align, allowing for a more authentic and impactful exchange of ideas.

To see how communities influence innovation and partnerships, you must also find key influencers. These communities come in two types: structured and stable or unstructured and dynamic. It is easy to recognize the leaders in structured communities, not so easy in the unstructured ones.

"In short, for many businesses, everything is changing: their customers, their competitors, their business models. They will have to reinvent themselves to operate in a completely different environment. As the borders between sectors fade, businesses are organizing into new, more dynamic configurations, centered not on the way things have always been done, but on people's needs."

–VENKAT ATLURI AND MIKLÓS DIETZ, THE ECOSYSTEM ECONOMY (HOBOKEN, NJ: JOHN WILEY & SONS , 2022)

Communities are often a significant influence on business decision-makers and the way they connect with partners. Today's decision-makers are more educated, know their customers, and cannot afford to waste time.

Let's explore the different types of communities, some traditional and others emerging. Which of these organizations are you working with already?

- *Trade Associations*

- *Local or Role-Based Organized Communities* with like-minded professionals

  - *Online Groups for Like-Minded Users; example: Reddit, Facebook*

  - *Peer Groups for Small Business Owners; example: Vistage, WEConnect*

  - *Peer Groups for Women Executives; example: Chief*

- *General Business Groups* with seminars and events

- *Industry-Specific Publications:* Webinars, podcasts, industry publications

- *Member-Built Communities:* Those who build their own communities of customers, prospects, and influencers

- *Vendor-Supplier-Led Communities*

- *Interest-Specific Communities*

Know what keeps your partners and the ecosystem up at night!

The way to identify your specific adjacent opportunities is to see how customers and suppliers are spending their time and finding out what keeps them up at night. In other words, your customers/suppliers and their community navigation will show the easy path to adjacencies.

In this book, for the sake of practical application and action let's focus on your communities. This strategy is the third critical tenet to your success in an ecosystem and with a partner growth strategy.

Chris Zook, in *Beyond the Core* (his follow-on book to his original *Profit from the Core*), explores a growth strategy through business adjacencies.[3] Adjacencies may be geographical, or expansion of services to current customers. These adjacencies carry less risk than diversification into unrelated businesses, yet they can create a significant competitive advantage because they stem directly from what the company already knows and does best.

Communities can be created by people, by companies, by your company, or by an association or consortium. They can be online, face to face, or hybrid. They take many shapes and sizes.

Here are five questions to determine what mix of communities is right for your needs:

Ask Yourself

1 What is your community strategy?

2 What communities do you need to have?

3 Which communities should you prioritize?

4 If you are a company CEO or executive, what communities could differentiate you?

5 In which communities are you a facilitator, and in which a participant?

Frank Vitagliano, a long-time tech industry executive and former CEO of a Managed Service Provider (MSP), a technology vendor and now CEO of the Global Tech Distribution Council, said, "The future

---

3   Chris Zook, *Beyond the Core: Expand Your Market without Abandoning Your Roots* (Boston, MA: Harvard Business School Press, 2004).

is about the ecosystem working together with a sense of community. And it's all about business value and trusting relationships."

A community strategy, just like a joint plan, should be simple. At AchieveUnite, we advise clients to pilot community initiatives that they believe they want to manage, and to experiment and try public and industry communities before making large commitments.

"Communities are grown organically with members' perceived value and relationships not manufactured. They must be natural and not too hard for the participant to become a part of. The reality is, different parts of the ecosystem will add value across the entire life cycle of the customer. Ensuring that you can tap into that value, and that the individual partner receives reciprocal value is what creates a fully functioning ecosystem."

–MICHELLE HODGES, GLOBAL VP, PARTNERS, IVANTI

Community involvement used to be taken for granted. Now, all partners must deliberately plan the communities they engage with, facilitate, or lead. Check out the example on the left, which shows a small business owner's community connection. On the right, you have a blank space to map out your own communities. You can organize them by location, strategy, solution, or role. Remember this is important for your organization as a strategy and for yourself personally. If you are in a leadership position or desire/aspire to be in a leadership position, you need communities. Everyone needs their own source of information, groups with similar passions, and trusted friends and business colleagues.

Start with your Community Needs Worksheet to determine which ones may be best for you:

Ask Yourself

Your Community Needs Worksheet:

Example

What communities can/will you participate with?

"The more common the need in many ways, the easier it is to build the community. The wider the group, the more diverse the group, the harder it is. And if you don't passionately care about the community members, you shouldn't be the orchestrator."

–ROD BAPTIE

Traditional groups like associations provide a set of industry education, certifications, and opportunities to share best practices. The lines of associations, media companies, events companies, and vendor communities are often blurring—so it's important to be clear on what you want from the community, and who you want to interact with. Many of the new opportunities surfacing in the B2B environment are coming from unstructured communities and events. Ad hoc personal relationships and access to internet-supplied perspective are the nontraditional sources.

Case Study in Action:

Why True Partnering in every facet of business is required globally and across industries

I had the opportunity to interview Elizabeth Vazquez. Elizabeth lives the system of partnering in all her work every day around the world; and leads a powerful global community as well.

In an interconnected global market, partnering is not just beneficial—it's essential.

Now inclusivity is not just a buzzword but a business imperative, WEConnect International emerges as a beacon of progress. At the helm is Elizabeth A. Vazquez, whose vision of economic empowerment for women transcends borders and barriers. This case study will delve into how WEConnect International, under Vazquez's leadership, has created a thriving global network, connecting women-owned businesses with significant buyers across the world. With a presence in over 130 countries and a reach that covers nearly 90 percent of the global population, the organization has been pivotal in certifying and elevating women-owned enterprises, aiding them in accessing capital, markets, and opportunities on an unprecedented scale. Beyond mere transactions, WEConnect International's mission is to forge partnerships that are the cornerstone of societal advancement, embodying the intricate dance of aligning goals, managing expectations, and building relationships that are as resilient as they are rewarding. Her goal: economic empowerment for women through access to capital, markets, and opportunities. WEConnect International stands out by certifying women-owned businesses and linking them with major buyers, fostering a global community that spans over 130 countries.

"The WEConnect International's WECommunity supports and promotes women-owned businesses based in over 130 countries representing 87.6 percent of the world's population, including local support and certification in over 50 countries across the Americas, Asia, Europe, the Middle East, and Africa. The organization also helps to develop the capacity of its large member buyers to source more products and services from underutilized suppliers, especially women-owned businesses globally. WEConnect International member buyers spend over $3 trillion per year on products and services.

Partnerships form the backbone of societal progress. Understanding the ecosystem—how governments, private sectors, and societies interplay—is the first step to crafting transformative alliances. Challenges in partnerships often stem from communication and goal setting. It's about managing expectations, aligning visions, and plotting a course together with clear accountability and timelines. Recognizing when to persevere, adjust, or even walk away from a partnership is as important as forging one. At WEConnect International, managing myriad relationships and strategic partnerships is complex and dynamic.

WEConnect International's mission thrives on its diverse and dynamic partnerships, enabling the organization to support women suppliers and member buyers globally. By educating and uniting stakeholders across all sectors, WEConnect International streamlines the path to engaging with women-led businesses—urging the world to leverage its purchasing power to make a meaningful impact.

Partnerships are the fabric of our society in this next era. We must first understand the intricacies of the ecosystem: how citizens perform with government, how regional governments benefit society and the private sector, and the intricacies of how society works. Once we know what the ecosystem looks like, then we're able to change it and be creative in how we build impactful partnerships for impact at scale.

What is critical for a partnership to be successful? Listening is a very critical aspect for all successful partnerships. You must first seek to understand what it is that a potential partner does and why they do it. What motivates them? How do they serve their communities? Then you try to figure out how you can add value to what they're doing. How can you align their purpose or mission, or goals with your purpose, mission, or goals?

Determining how to align yourself without losing yourself is key. You don't want to try to become all things to all people. So, you look for that overlap where what they do complements what you do. And in that sweet spot you can build an amazing partnership, communicating firmly and setting both short-term and long-term goals. You must properly manage expectations. You must know where you are individually, and where you are together, and agree on where you're going together. And then you must work backward with appreciative inquiry and say, OK, this is where we are and we're going together, so what do we need to do to get to where we want to go? And then we must agree on those next steps. There must be an alignment and ownership on both sides: accountability, accountability, accountability. And a clear timetable with deliverables is required.

Once you establish a partnership, it is important to maintain that relationship and check in regularly to make sure all the stakeholders are happy with the relationship and are getting what they need out of it and if not, it is important to create space for direct feedback and adjustments. You also must know when a partnership is not working and when to adjust or when to walk away. You can waste so much time if there is no alignment or the timing is wrong. No one wants to fail and so sometimes we try to make something work for too long.

We use a partnership review and segmentation process. We ask, how important is the partnership? We can't prioritize them all equally. Therefore, we must prioritize different partnerships for different reasons at different times.

Partners must be particularly careful with payment terms—timing, invoicing, currencies, etc.—especially noting that the relative value of currencies and other assets can change over time. The bottom line is that when money is involved in a partnership, having actual contracts and not just a handshake or an MOU is critical. This is how you minimize surprises and maximize your ability to anticipate and address challenging topics in a calm environment before you enter a structured partnership.

In fact, we spend a lot of our time educating and connecting ecosystem stakeholders across the public sector, private sector, and civil society. These strategic partner ecosystem investments are how we make it as easy as possible for the world to find and buy from innovative women suppliers of products and services, and I hope everyone joins our movement and leverages their purchasing power to buy more from women and change our world."

This is an excerpt from the full interview on the importance of partnerships across countries and small business. For the full interview, visit: https://www.achieveunite.com/partneringsuccessbookresources/.

Case Study: Mindset AI

This next case study demonstrates at time of publication leading-edge methods and sources of community using AI. This leaves many questions for us to grapple with—what are AI agents capable of and their limitations? What is the role of humans? What happens to team dynamics and partner dynamics when an AI agent becomes your new coworker? One thing is certain: it's never been so important to build trust with your team, partners, and ecosystem because AI in community, in ecosystem partnerships, and in solutions is going to become the norm for growth and time to market acceleration.

Enabling new sources of community and new ways to build community leveraging AI: Barrie Hadfield, CEO of Mindset AI, a partner of AchieveUnite in the learning and artificial intelligence space, has innovated dramatically with AI and community.

He shares: *"Let's say you were asked to accelerate partnerships and help companies grow their businesses together in partnership with other organizations. Imagine a world where all of you can participate in the community leveraging AI, automate the manual workflows, and simplify and streamline people's efforts so they can focus on growth and their interests of these partnering relationships. Humans get to learn, interact, and build businesses, and intelligence for growth is right at their fingertips. And we can help grow the organizations' people much faster with these critical growth strategies developed using human interaction, community, and AI."*

AI is not just a tool but a team member, integral to driving business growth and partnership synergy. Hadfield envisions a future where AI's capability to automate and enhance workflows allows humans to focus on strategic growth areas, fostering learning, interaction, and business development. However, this integration of AI into the core of business operations raises pivotal questions about the role of humans in a new AI-augmented workplace, the evolving nature of team and partner dynamics, and the implications of AI agents as coworkers.

Should You Build or Participate in a Community—or Both?

If a community exists providing what you can provide, should you compete with them? You might be better off not creating a community, instead joining an existing one in a meaningful way by becoming a valuable contributor.

Creating a community is not for the fainthearted. It requires a long-term perspective. It often takes two to five years for a community to be introduced, grow, and actively prosper. It's important to commit and resource properly a community and ensure you can maintain and continuously invest and improve the value for the members.

Rod Baptie: Top Five Community Fundamentals for Building or Participating in a Community

1. *Create a community for the community members and not for the leader. The community must be about the members.* The mistake most community originators make is believing they know what the community wants. When in fact, only the community members know what the community wants.

2. *When considering communities, have a solid agreed-upon plan that answers these questions:*

   □ What is my community landscape and what makes it unique?

   □ What is the current community competitive landscape of the community and how will your community compete?

   □ How do the community goals mesh with the members' goals? The more overlap the better.

   □ How are you going to create something that's meaningful for your targeted membership (compelling content, respected peers, and attractive venues)?

Balance structure with member-to-member orientation. Since communities are not top-down and not highly structured because they are member-to-member oriented, you need to have the right level of structure in place for communities to still have their freedom to interact yet have some sense of a central purpose.

3. *Commit for the long term.* You might be better off not creating a new community, but joining a community that already exists and becoming a valuable contributor to it. You can't create a valued community overnight. You must be passionate about what you're doing. You must be passionate about the members. And you must really care about the community and the value that it brings. Always improve, innovate, and evolve. When you get a rating of nine out of ten, or you get ten out of ten, you cannot be satisfied. When the same people come back to the next session, the ratings will be lower unless you innovate. You must be constantly looking at what you're doing, constantly looking at what people want, constantly looking at how you're doing it and how you can improve it.

4. *Be very specific about who can and can't be a member and preserve confidentiality.* Depending on the kind of community you're trying to create, you've got to be very specific about who can and who can't be a member. To provide peer value for the community, you need commonality and often some level of exclusivity. Build the muscles of radical candor and *trustworthiness.* Preserve confidentiality. Create a safe, trusting space for people to talk and interact.

5. *Create a community circle of value.* The more people you speak to, the more people talk about what you are doing, and the value you are providing, which creates opportunities for influence. The more people you bring into what you're doing, the more you're going to understand what they want and the more successful you're going to be.

Communities of influence (partnerships, associations, peer groups) are valued colleagues that cannot be controlled but can be influenced.

-Rod Baptie,
Owner, Baptie & Company

These rules of community apply regardless of the type of community or purpose.

Key Considerations Checklist

- [ ] **Communities are for the benefits of the members**

- [ ] **Communities must be future-oriented**

- [ ] **Customers must participate actively in the communities**

- [ ] **Communities have different value for a supplier, a partner, and a customer**

- [ ] **New technologies like - AI, IPT, 3D Printing, Virtual Reality - are reshaping communities**

- [ ] **Communities should be viewed with a long-term Partner Lifetime Value lens.**

Looking ahead, the challenge for organizations will be to navigate these evolving ecosystems with agility and foresight. The integration of new technologies and the constant reshaping of communities demand a flexible and participatory approach, where mutual benefits are the cornerstone of any partnership.

The lessons laid out in this chapter are clear: Embrace the community as an extension of your business, nurture it with purpose and passion, and let it be the guiding force behind your innovation and strategic partnerships. By doing so, you'll be well-equipped to harness the ever-expanding opportunities of the Ecosystem Economy, where businesses and communities thrive in unison, creating a sustainable and prosperous future for all.

Key Takeaways from Chapter 11

1. Engagement and the strategic development of partner communities are critical for business competitiveness in the modern ecosystem economy. Organizations must move beyond transactional relationships to foster communities that drive innovation, learning, and collective growth.

2. The success of an ecosystem hinges on the ability to adapt and collaborate. Real-world examples, like those from WEConnect International, highlight how understanding the interplay between different ecosystem stakeholders can lead to sustainable growth and significant economic empowerment.

3. Integrating advanced technologies such as artificial intelligence can revolutionize how communities communicate, learn, and grow together. AI offers new ways to enhance the efficiency and effectiveness of community-based strategies, ultimately accelerating partnership development and business growth.

Partnering Road Map–Action Steps

- *Identify and engage with partners who* share both your immediate goals and long-term vision to ensure a sustained and mutual commitment to growth. Select your communities wisely and reevaluate annually the goals and values. If you invest in a community, be deliberate to maximize the opportunities afforded to you.

- *Transition from transactional interactions to cultivating deep-seated partnerships* that prioritize mutual success and longevity over short-term gains. Ensure that you have a set of personal communities for your own interests and goals; and leverage the community planning for your organization's community planning strategy.

- Be sure you understand the partner dynamics in your business relationships. Analyze and align with your partners' business models to find common ground for collaboration, essential for driving strategic growth and acceleration.

CHAPTER 12

WRAP UP: THE SYSTEM FOR PARTNERING SUCCESS

"Individually we are one drop, but together we are an ocean."

–RYUNOSUKE SATORO

We aim for this book to have provided a thorough understanding of the key aspects of effective partnering and the foundational principles of successful partnerships. Ultimately, our goal is to emphasize the significance of long-term behavioral change. This process extends beyond mere knowledge acquisition and requires ongoing dedication. Embracing a commitment to continual learning is crucial for navigating today's professional landscapes adeptly.

Additionally, fostering a culture of collaboration within your organization is paramount. This entails integrating collaboration deeply into your business's identity, fostering innovation and synergies across all levels. By instilling a mindset of continual learning and partnership within the organizational framework, companies can gain a strategic advantage in collaborative endeavors. Therefore, it is essential for lifelong learning and the cultivation of a collaborative mindset to be integral components of any organization's partnership strategy.

Partnering Uniters and Deflators

Since partnering in some form is fast becoming a must for every organization small or large, the processes supporting the Business Acceleration and Relationship Development dimensions are critical. Partner-related processes need to reinforce the partnership, not make it more challenging to work together.

Partnering Uniters are natural forces that accelerate and reinforce partnering connections. These forces are further aligned with the Three Dimensions of partnering. Conversely, Partnering Deflators are roadblocks to partnering success. These roadblocks can hold back partnering progress for months or even years.

This Partnering Uniter checklist offers you an opportunity to determine what strengths you can build into your partnerships and identify your most significant gaps.

UNITERS	STATUS TODAY (RED/YELLOW/ GREEN)	KEY IMPROVEMENT NEEDS
Relationship Development		
Complementary Values and Cultures. We have laid out the values and cultures of each organization and identified the areas of complements as well as gaps.		
Trust Profile Assessments. We have conducted a PQi® workshop to understand each other's profiles.		

Personal Motivations of Leaders. We have conducted leader-to-leader workshops to ensure that the long-term objectives of the partnership are established, documented, and hard commitments solidified.			
Open Access to Strategic Information. We have discussed and agreed to share key confidential information relevant to success.			
Business Acceleration			
Growth. We have agreed to a set of mutual revenue objectives and have established a cadence for health checks.			
Resource Sharing (People, Systems, Financing). We have outlined key shared resources and clearly defined our expected results.			
Innovation—Joint Offerings. We have reviewed three to five end client opportunities and agreed on a joint needs assessment and/or joint offerings.			
Common Success Metrics. We have identified a few non-revenue leading indicator unified goals, which will form the basis for evaluating the partnership.			
Intersecting Business Models. In addition to documenting our similarities, we have clearly discussed areas where our business models diverge or do NOT align.			
Community Orchestration			
Current Community Comparisons. We have identified communities that we have in common and ways that we can both benefit from community participation.			
Joint Community Initiation. We have identified how we can develop our own mutually beneficial communities.			

DEFLATORS	STATUS TODAY (R/Y/G)	IMPROVE-MENTS
Relationship Development		
Communications Breakdown. Our top executives have not met with partners to understand the synergies that exist.		
Functional Misalignment. My organization is not 100 percent+ committed to partner-centric strategy or not clear about where we leverage partners demonstrating mixed signals to partners.		
One-Sided Information Sharing. My organization asks for partner information without sharing equally valuable data.		
Business Acceleration		
Myopic Growth. My organization is primarily concerned with its own growth and seems not to care much about the partners' success.		
Lack of Involvement in Partner's Business Improvements. My organization is not concerned about using its resources to improve partners' businesses.		
Willingness of Product Development to Collaborate with Partners. Product engineers keep new product ideas and plans from partners; and partner feedback is not built into the product development process.		
Awareness of Partner's Customer Experience. We have a lack of willingness to help partners with their customer opportunities and not compete with them.		
Community Orchestration		
Community Ignorance. My organization does not recognize the impact and influence of communities in our partner ecosystems.		

These exercises and checklists are tools you can reference again and again as you build successful partnerships. Building partnering into your company's DNA has successful acceleration benefits externally, and ripple effects for your teams and yourself.

Executive Summary for the System for Partnering Success

- The recognition of the importance of partnering as a strategic imperative.

- The building of authentic and trusting relationships, personally and institutionally, with your most strategic partners.

- Conducting the necessary research to understand your partner's business goals and personal aspirations.

- Tapping into your peripheral vision to see what communities are influencing your partners; leverage those communities for joint benefit.

A Commitment to Partnering North Star, KPIs, and Policies is the most important step to address. Without commitment from the top of the partnering organizations, efforts will fail, partner people will get frustrated and leave, and a revenue growth opportunity will evaporate. Here are a few tips to demonstrate the commitment to partnering:

- Add partnering to the values of the organization.

- Feature partner success in the press, on the organization's website, and in organizational meetings. Talk the talk and walk the talk.

- Drive all C-level executives, not just the sales leader, to spend time meeting with partner executives. Encourage the executives to visit them at their offices and headquarter locations.

- Include partnering investment as part of the organization's strategic planning process on par with your Capital Plan.

- Articulate and display partner metrics throughout the organization.

The *Relationship Trust* dimension requires a conscious effort and a set of metrics to verify progress.

- PQi is an essential tool in the development of personal trust, team trust, interfunctional trust, and interorganizational alignment and trust.

- Trust is a foundational element in all aspects of partnering: Inside the walls of the partnering organizations and outside. PQi builds a natural commitment and language for authentic partnering.

- The need for trusting relationships accelerates during times of change. As the partnering relationships get more complex, it will be important to move faster with partnering, and to innovate in partnering. Trust can be especially jeopardized during rapid change and therefore must be a conscious effort. One of my favorite sayings to remember is "Trust is earned in drops and lost in buckets."

The *Business Acceleration* dimension starts with an understanding of the partner's business model and aspirations.

- Relationships without Business Accelerator are friendships, not partnerships.

- Business Acceleration *for external organization partnering* is connected through the 5Ps of partnering success. The Five "P"s of Partnering bind you with partners with common goals and success metrics.

- Set aggressive partnering goals with your "best fit" partners, plan regularly, conduct periodic health checks, and remember to always celebrate success.

The *Community Orchestration* dimension shows us that partnership community points of influence need to be identified and understood.

- Communities cannot be controlled.

- As an investment, business leaders need to decide which of these communities are worth membership, whether the organization needs to build its own community or communities, and which communities are not a priority based on resources available.

- In general, companies need a balanced and multipronged approach to communities.

Final Case Study in Action

Jeff Taylor, Worldwide Channel Marketing Leader at Lenovo, sees customer and integrator relationships in different parts of the world and in different business models every day. While building interpersonal trust is critical to building long-term relationships with these partners, Jeff realizes that success requires more investment, beyond enabling transactions, to achieve the potential of partnerships.

When asked about his attention on building relationships with partners, Jeff said, "How would you like to have access to one million incremental salespeople that sit in partners' organizations? Would these incremental sales resources be worth an investment in partnerships?" When he presents the opportunity for partner investment in the context of incremental salespeople, suddenly, we think differently and realize quickly the vast and depth of power in Partner LifeTime Value partnering.

Jeff authored *Bigger Than the Widget*. His book lists the four relationship principles needed to establish a branded connection with partners and customers. This connection needs to be both a personal one and a business connection. The four are:

- *Mutual Commitment*—Whether good times or bad, the commitment must be strong enough to weather any rough storms. Over time, this commitment level becomes even more dominant.

- *Mutual Growth*—Effective partnerships are bound together by a common passion for the success of the partnership.

- *Mutual Profitability*—Each participant in the partnership expects to gain something over and above what they could accomplish alone. And additional profitability becomes a source of funding for even more success investments.

- *Brand*—Each relationship has a unique set of behaviors and expectations. Recognizing the uniqueness calls for a customized approach to each partner's needs and potential.

Jeff summarized his view of long-term success with partners in one word, "mutuality." If you become trusted with partners, are open and transparent, and are committed to mutual success, access to the one million salespeople will be your return on partnership investments.

Is your System for Partnering Success ready to be launched, does it need to be refined, or perhaps completely revamped? It doesn't matter if you are a CEO, CFO, CRO, partner or franchise owner, partner manager, a sales rep, a product officer, or an entrepreneur, mastering the system for partnering is the gift that keeps on giving. Every person and organization is on a different launch pad. Following this system will ensure that you maximize your partner ecosystem and relationships, your Partner LifeTime Value®, and that you accelerate your success in the future.

At AchieveUnite, we have dedicated ourselves to crafting a blueprint for partnership excellence that has been instrumental in the growth and success of hundreds of organizations. Our comprehensive education programs have honed the skills of over eight thousand professionals from more than three hundred companies at the time of publication, including executives and partnering and sales teams, by fostering a deep understanding of successful collaboration techniques.

With over three thousand certified Partner Performance Advisors to date, we take pride in our proven track record of accelerating the journey to partnership success—shaving off between six and twenty-four months for many of our clients. Our strategies have been pivotal in elevating historically direct companies from zero to up to 50 percent in partner-generated revenue, ensuring they not only thrive but lead in the AI-driven marketplace. In addition, our programs have accelerated teamwork and high-performing partnerships and helped organizations achieve 200 percent growth over a two-year period.

Whether you're looking to ignite growth in a nascent partnership program or seeking to revitalize mature alliances, AchieveUnite is equipped to propel your people and your company forward. We are committed to transforming your partnership vision into measurable success and would be privileged to partner with you on this journey. Let's unlock the full potential of your collaborations together.

SYSTEM FOR PARTNERING SUCCESS

PARTNERING NORTH STAR

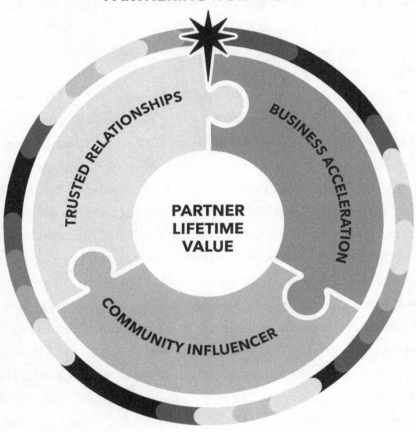

AchieveUnite 3 Pillars Solutions

Maximizing Partner Lifetime Value® = Revenue and Growth Acceleration

People Development

- Leaders/Coaches
- Partner Managers: Sellers
- Partner Teams
- Executives
- Cross Functional Teams

Advisory Services

- Partnering Strategy
- Accelerate Partnering Success
- Build/Update your Program
- Advise Leadership

Growth Catalyst Programs

- Events, Workshops, Keynotes
- Partner Selection
- Recruitment

Let us know how we can support your Strategic Partnership journey. You can find us at https://www.achieveunite.com/partnering successbookresources/

LinkedIn: AchieveUnite.

RESOURCES

Your Organization's Partnering Growth DNA Assessment

Your Organization's Partnering Growth DNA

Take the assessment below and rate your and your organization's Partnering Growth DNA. You have two alternatives as you complete the assessment:

1. Use the questions below, filling in the template you will find at https://www.achieveunite.com/partneringsuccessbookresources/ to identify your most significant strengths as well as gaps.

2. Go to the System for Partnering Success site at https://www.achieveunite.com/partneringsuccessbookresources/ and complete the assessment. When you do so, we will provide you with a system-generated diagnostic with your strength

and gaps. Your information will be held in the strictest confidence.

Question #1—Why is partnering essential in the rapidly changing digital, agile, and hybrid business world?

A. My organization has a clear bias to building partnerships in defined markets.

B. My organization's partners are developing more sophisticated and capable products and services, necessitating a shift in our strategy.

C. My partners are being more selective in traditional relationships as they expand their ecosystems into adjacencies.

D. My organization has a priority on developing and measuring extraordinary partner experience.

Question #2—For successful business partnering, what is expected from each function in an organization (sales, finance, legal, operations, product development, and marketing)?

A. My organization's sales strategy and routes to end markets are well-defined and adhered to, without exception.

B. All my organization's support functions are aware of the partnering success metrics and are committed to partner success.

C. My organization's CEO, CFO, COO, and CMO regularly visit our partners to show their interest in the partner's businesses.

D. My organization views partner suggestions seriously and has a process to solicit partner ideas for implementation.

Question #3—How can you use your partnering profile (Partnering Quotient index—PQi) to increase your effectiveness and build trusted relationships?

A. Building cross-functional relationships is a competency for me and my organization, in general.

B. It would be very helpful to me to know my partnering personality, its strengths, and its weaknesses.

C. In mergers, acquisitions, reorganizations, and new initiatives, it is important to form a new team chemistry quickly.

D. Building a trusted relationship with partners is the first step in making a difference in the partnership results.

Question #4—What trust-building techniques do you find most effective for you when working with internal and external partners?

A. I am not afraid of appearing vulnerable when dealing with my partners.

B. When meeting with partners, I always ask probing questions and listen for meaning more than I talk.

C. I ask my partners to call me on my cell at any time, 24×7, if they have a concern or if I can be of help.

D. I constantly look for opportunities where I can provide nontransactional assistance to demonstrate that I go above and beyond the basics.

Question #5—What importance do you and your organization place on building successful partnerships for the long term (Partner LifeTime Value®)?

A. My organization has a rigorous process for partner selection, onboarding, and engineering one-hundred-day successes.

B. My QBRs place equal emphasis and time on the immediate operations (revenue, quality, timeliness) and the strategy (new offerings, new markets under consideration, and resource planning).

C. Partner defections or drop-offs in business activity are taken seriously in my organization, drawing the attention of top management.

D. I can define Partner LifeTime Value® in my own terms with clear examples.

Question #6—What are the characteristics that you use to select your ideal partner segments?

A. My organization has a quantifiable, ideal partner profile backed by years of success data.

B. Part of my organization's ideal partner profile is the partner decision-makers' willingness to be open to share as much as we are.

C. My organization segments partners (suppliers, integrators, customers) based on their fit and potential for future accelerated success.

D. Our partners are growing revenue faster than the markets they serve.

Question #7—What do you know about your more strategic business partners to be an asset in the delivery of value to the relationship?

- A. I have taken time to fully understand my partner's business operations and priorities.

- B. I have an open personal relationship with the decision-makers, to include joint sales calls, product planning, common staged events, and press releases.

- C. I know how and when my partner is making strategic investments and am often asked for my opinion.

- D. My partner decision-makers have shared confidential information with me.

Question #8—What techniques do you have to earn for a "Seat at the Partner's Table" and then to keep this "Seat"?

- A. I have shown an appropriate level of curiosity about how my partner does planning and makes tough decisions.

- B. I have offered nontraditional resources from my organization to assist my partner in his business processes (budgeting, marketing campaigns, technical support, or sales training).

- C. I have proven to my partner that I can be trusted with sensitive information.

- D. I make commitments to my partner and always honor these commitments.

Question #9—How do you understand, influence, and sometimes lead the communities your partners participate in?

A. I show my partner that I value his/her time and do not suggest any community participation that I have not investigated thoroughly.

B. I respect my partner's need to participate in communities beyond my reach but offer my help with the preparation should it be needed.

C. I explore, with my partner, communities that may provide future value, while I help in the value assessment of current communities.

D. At the invitation of my partner, I participate in community activities, jointly or as a representative.

Question #10—How do you use the three partnering dimensions (Relationship Development, Business Accelerator, and Community Orchestration) to propel your partnering success?

A. I understand that building long-lasting partnerships is not an accidental happening and I prepare myself for each partner interaction with partner success paramount.

B. I have a multiyear commitment to my role in creating success for my partners.

C. My organization's commitment to partnering success includes a personal relationship and a business connection that are stronger than any of my competitors.

D. Realizing that the business world is changing more rapidly than ever, I am constantly looking for insight that will help my partner's agility.

Glossary of Terms: System for Partnering Success

- *Co-Investment*: Identifying the supplier's operational resources and assets that support the integrator's needs or customer's needs for growth, expense reduction, and quality improvement. The "co" implies that the sharing is bilateral going across organizational boundaries in supply-side and demand-side directions.

- *Ecosystem of Partners*: Dynamic communities of businesses combining respective experiences, skills, and resources to deliver unique capabilities with greater speed and efficiency than could be generated otherwise.

- *Intersection Planning*: The supplier's partner team joins the integrator or customer's planning cycle and calendar, not enforcing the supplier's process and timing. Each participant identified needs and opportunities providing mutual value for strategic benefit implementing co-investment tactics.

- *Joint Value Proposition*: Combining the products and services of the supplier and the integrator to create a new offering not possible with either party operating alone.

- *Natural Partner Fit*: Involves the process to segment partners that are aligned with the supplier or integrator on growth aspirations with a shared vision of the success opportunities.

- *Partner Life Cycle*: The stages of engagement between suppliers and integrators. While each industry relies on a variety of models with numerous levels, each should include a detection or identification phase, followed by engagement or recruitment before moving into the onboarding and then nurturing

197

or management stages. Suppliers and integrators utilize this process to track progress and provide support where needed to ensure the success of their partnerships.

- *Partner LifeTime Value*®: The amount of revenue and profit potential a partnership represents over the relationship lifetime.

- *Partnering Growth DNA*: A partnering, highly collaborative ethos and value that serves as the dominant cultural trait of an individual, team, or organization.

- *Value Measurement index*: A measure of an organization's partnering motivation and partnering capabilities. The higher the Value Maturity, the more successful its partnering relationships are.

- *Partner Success Planning*: The activity where partner-facing teams engage with each other to review the business metrics, reevaluate priorities, and enhance the relationship. This activity is focused on what each partner needs to succeed in the relationship and documents the joint commitment to success.

- *Partnering Trust*: The intention and act of developing mutually satisfying and effective relationships based on competence, integrity, and benevolence for a stated purpose. Partnering Trust can be built between two individuals or within groups of teams, organizations, clients, suppliers, customers, students, and/or communities. When Partnering Trust is high, the result is a relationship or environment that is safe, resilient, open, high performing, and inclusive.

- *Partnering Quotient index (PQi®)*: The measure of an individual or team's personal partnering profile and propensity for developing trusted partnerships.

- *Recurring Revenue*: A predictable, repeating income stream. Unlike a discrete sales transaction, a consumption-based or subscription services agreement, flowing on a monthly, quarterly, or annual basis.

- *System for Partnering Success*: A managed process for the development and execution of partnerships that results in a successful outcome over time. The System consists of three dimensions: relationship development, business relevance, and community orchestration.

- *Vertizontal*: Combining vertical and horizontal business models into one structure. Rationale for partnering, which combines specialization in each into a collaborative relationship.

THANK YOU FOR READING *PARTNERING SUCCESS: THE FORCE MULTIPLIER TO ACHIEVE EXPONENTIAL GROWTH*

I hope you found valuable insights and inspiration in this book. Your journey to building and sustaining successful strategic partnerships and alliances for life is just beginning, and I'm here to support you every step of the way.

Share Your Feedback

I would love to hear your thoughts! Share your feedback on social media using our hashtags and handles:

Hashtags:
- #PartneringSuccessBook
- #AchieveUnite

Handles:
- **LinkedIn:** @Theresa Caragol | @AchieveUnite
- **Instagram:** @TheresaCaragol

Access Exclusive Resources

- For a downloadable **cool freebie** and additional resources please visit: www.achieveunite.com/partneringsuccessbookresources/

- To book **Theresa Caragol** to speak at your event, please send an email to theresa@achieveunite.com or info@achieveunite.com

Write a Review

If you enjoyed this book, please consider writing a review with your honest impressions on Amazon, Goodreads, or the platform of your choosing. Your feedback is incredibly valuable for helping independent authors like me to reach a wider audience.

Stay Connected

Thank you for being a part of our community and for your commitment to achieving exponential growth through strategic partnerships.

Resources Here:

Let's Connect!

Printed in the USA
CPSIA information can be obtained
at www.ICGtesting.com
JSHW021231291024
72565JS00002B/5

9 781642 257588